Touching the Past
Archaeology 5-14

Touching the Past
Archaeology 5-14

edited by Elizabeth and Neil Curtis

SCOTTISH CHILDREN'S PRESS

published 1996
Scottish Children's Press
Unit 14, Leith Walk Business Centre
130 Leith Walk
Edinburgh EH6 5DT
Tel:0131-555 5950 Fax 0131-555 5018

British Library Cataloguing in Publication Data
A catalogue record for this book is available from the British Library

ISBN: 1 899827 63 3

Publication sponsored by:

HISTORIC SCOTLAND

Contents

Foreword

This book grew out of the *Touching the Past* seminar held in Marischal Museum on 17th June 1995. The subtitle of the seminar 'Archaeology 5-14' referred to the 5-14 National Guidelines which were published between 1991 and 1993 to provide curricular guidance to schools teaching children between the ages of 5 and 14. Largely due to its contentious nature, one of the last documents to be published was 'Environmental Studies'. It is the most obvious home of archaeology as it encompasses history, geography, technology and the study of society. Although the Guidelines are at an early stage in their implementation, the demands of schools are already changing. The importance of an investigative approach to learning has been underlined, giving children the opportunity for experiences outwith the classroom in place of a reliance on text books.

With the relevance of archaeological approaches emphasised by curricular developments, the seminar aimed to bring together archaeologists and teachers to share examples of good practice and to consider ways in which resources could be tailored to suit the needs of schools. One of the most striking features of the meeting was the number of participants who were already providing high-quality archaeological experiences for schools, but who did not know of the work of other people elsewhere in Scotland. As a result, the original intention to publish the proceedings of the meeting was overtaken by a desire to include the work of others who had not given formal presentations or who had been unable to attend. Thanks to the generosity of Historic Scotland, the Council for British Archaeology, Scottish Museum Archaeologists and the Kilmartin House Trust, it has been possible to publish these papers in a much substantial and attractive form than would otherwise have been possible.

The contributors come from a variety of backgrounds: teachers, school advisors, archaeologists working for excavation units and others working in museums, with a wide range of experiences. Despite this and the diversity of approaches, a number of features can be seen linking the papers in this volume. In all cases, children are offered the chance to encounter evidence for life in the past, developing their abilities to plan, collect evidence, ask questions and discuss their conclusions. As well as the investigative skills which these activities develop, the opportunities for personal discovery and excitement that archaeology offers is apparent in all the chapters.

This book represents the early stages of a dialogue between archaeologists and teachers. Hopefully, this will continue so that archaeologists will be able to provide resources that increasingly match the needs of teachers. This will include making links to other resources and to popular class projects. This dialogue will also help archaeologists to become more involved in encouraging the use of archaeology in schools, taking part in curricular and staff development. After all, archaeologists and teachers have the same aim - to help children to make links between archaeological evidence and an understanding of people in the past.

Archaeology and schools

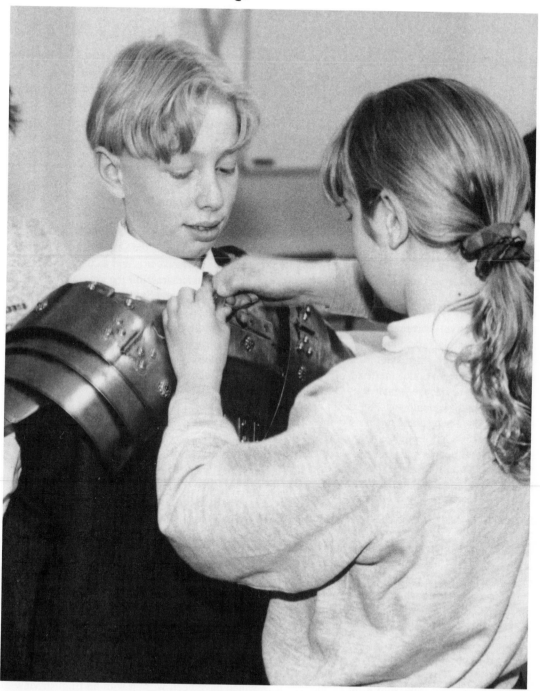

Problem solving with Roman armour at Perth Museum and Art Gallery

Using Archaeology in School

Elizabeth Curtis

Thanks to changes in the curriculum in Scottish primary schools brought about by the 5-14 Guidelines for Environmental Studies, the teaching of history and geography as separate disciplines is rapidly disappearing. This is not to say that neither are being taught, far from it! They are alive and well and working together as 'Understanding People in the Past' and 'Understanding People and Place'. From Skara Brae to Victorian Scotland, children are exploring space and time, and developing a wide range of knowledge and investigative skills.

As a teacher, I think *'understanding'* is the key to changes in teaching and learning. To achieve understanding, children have to be guided away from fact-focused learning towards exploratory and investigative learning. An archaeological approach to learning about the past is an effective way of achieving this aim. Like historians, archaeologists learn about the lives of people in the past. The evidence which they use is very varied, including monuments, museum objects, historical documents, and maps. To make any sense of the evidence, archaeologists have to be aware of other people's work, carry out their own fieldwork and, most importantly of all, to present their interpretation of the past in an accurate and interesting way to the public. I have consciously used archaeology in two projects carried out with classes of 8-9 year olds, one based on life in Skara Brae and the other on life in Scotland around the year 1300, with a focus on the growth of Aberdeen. In this paper, I will show how an archaeological approach can make projects in this aspect of Environmental Studies more challenging and enjoyable.

A project with a historical theme can be used to cover all the key features of 'Understanding People in the Past', and with a bit of thought it can include elements from 'Understanding People and Place'. A curriculum plan for a project with a historical theme uses a series of key features to provide the framework for the body of knowledge which children will learn by implementing the following five strands for social subjects.

- Planning
- Collecting Evidence
- Recording and Presenting
- Interpreting and Evaluating
- Developing Informed Attitudes

The use of archaeological evidence also has links to other areas of the curriculum, such as language, expressive arts and technology, but this paper will concentrate on the key features of the 5 -14 Environmental Studies Guidelines.

Understanding People in the Past
Studying people, events, and societies of significance in the past
There is currently debate about which people, events and societies should be considered to be of significance in the past. In the Guidelines the past has been divided into five periods:
- The Ancient World (pre 5th century AD)
- The Middle Ages (400-1450)
- Renaissance, Reformation and the Age of Discovery (1450-1700)
- The Age of Revolutions (1700-1900.)
- The Twentieth Century

Unlike the National Curriculum in England which specifies which topics are to be taught to each year group, the Guidelines offer great flexibility for schools. Unfortunately, this has frightened off many publishers from producing resources for Scottish schools as the potential market is so uncertain. As a result in many teachers, although wanting their projects to have a Scottish focus, having to rely on resources which have been written with an English view of which aspects of history are of greatest significance. The onus is therefore on resource

4

providers to be aware of what is being taught in schools, and so produce stimulating resources that have a local and a Scottish focus.

I chose Skara Brae as a focus for a study of the Ancient World (pre 5th Century AD). Well recorded excavations in the twentieth century have provided a wealth of information relating to life in the village at a time when farming had become established and bronze working was a known skill, while evidence from other sites in Orkney, such as the Ring of Brodgar and Maes Howe, help to provide a lively picture of life about 4000 years ago. The survival of Skara Brae has another significance. It helps to challenge children to consider why so much can be seen today. If the village had not been built almost entirely from stone, if it had not eventually been completely buried in the sand and if the sand had not shifted in the late 19th century, the evidence would have been very different. For comparison the class looked at evidence for contemporary in the North-East to reinforce the idea that people were also living in other parts of Scotland at the same time.

As a focus for the study of the Middle Ages in Scotland, I chose the time between the death of Alexander III and the crowning of Robert the Bruce. Historically this is an important period, encouraging the investigation of the cause and effect of the death of a king without a direct heir and the ensuing tussle for the throne. As the thread through the project, I chose the story of the attempt to bring the Maid of Norway to Scotland as Queen which, as told by Francis Mary Hendry in *Quest for a Maid*, provided a powerful narrative. The use of the novel helped provide a rich context for the discussion of alternative images of the past. Archaeologically it is an extremely rich period as many Scottish burghs have recently been excavated and children are often already familiar with castles and churches. In Aberdeen, the Urban Studies Centre and the City Archaeology Unit provide resources designed for children to find out about life in the medieval burgh. These are discussed elsewhere.

Developing an understanding of time and historical sequence

One of the first tasks in teaching a historical topic is to help children to develop an understanding of time and to set up a chronological framework for the project. While timelines are a popular visual way of showing the passing of time, I have found a vertical timeline particularly helpful. On a vertical timeline, the farther back in time an event in history is, the farther down the timeline it appears; just as during an excavation the most recent objects are usually found nearest the surface and the oldest lower down. To go back to Scotland at the time of Alexander III, I used a line calibrated in 100 year intervals to about 1000 years ago which was then adorned with photographs, maps and postcards marking things which the children recognised as coming from different times in the past. To travel back 4000 years a timeline with as few as three dates was appropriate: 'Now', '2000 years ago' and '4000 years ago'. It is important that children are involved in deciding which historic events and times should be included on the timeline. This helps children to see the relative positions in time of, for example, Victorians, Vikings and Romans. It also helps to create a continuum of time in the children's minds, and emphasises that the patch of time that they are studying comes either before or after the lives of other people.

Children can also make their own family trees, like the one shown below. Unlike a traditional family tree, this one starts at the top with a living tree, representing the child and the roots of the tree their ancestors. As with the timeline, each child can travel backwards in their own family history. Most children can trace as far back as their grandparents, some to great-grandparents and a few even farther. Creating family trees needs sensitivity and planning as there can be problems with some children if they are adopted, have a parent or a sibling who has died, or if there have been family separations. Creating a family tree helps to reinforce the children's understanding of the idea that other people and places have a past too.

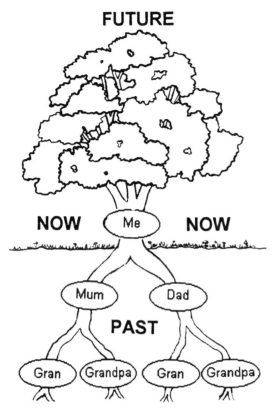

FUTURE

NOW Me **NOW**

PAST

Mum Dad

Gran Grandpa Gran Grandpa

A family tree

Developing an understanding of change and continuity and cause and effect
Historical fiction is invaluable in providing a framework for study and exploration. The characters in the story have their lives moulded by historical events, helping children to discuss cause and effect through the fictional narrative. In a similar way, by looking for blocked up windows or roof scars on a building, children can see tangible evidence for change and continuity.

Developing an understanding of the nature of historical evidence
It is crucially important to the development of an understanding of the nature of historical evidence that children recognise the difference between *primary evidence* - the real thing: a pot, a castle, an original manuscript or a standing stone - and *secondary evidence* - a picture, film, book, or facsimile of the real thing.

It is important to be aware of this at the planning stage so that primary evidence can be consciously included, as it is all too easy to rely on secondary evidence alone. I am fortunate, to be teaching in Aberdeen, because there is a wide range of primary resources specifically designed for use by children. Direct experience of objects and landscapes from the past helps children to understand something of the nature of historical evidence, and make them better able to pose questions and discuss other people's inter-pretation of the past. For example, a visit to Marischal Museum provided an excellent stimulus for discussion about decay, survival and changes over time. Why do different materials have different survival rates? Why have archaeologists found bronze axes and stone axe moulds, but not wooden shafts? Exploring a local cathedral , castle or street helps children to make tangible links to the past through the fabric of buildings. Children can make suggestions about why they were built in a particular place and consider how its position relative to other buildings has changed.

The bulk of children's learning, however, comes from secondary sources. As well as books and television, reconstructions of the past like 'Step into Medieval Aberdeen' is a secondary source which makes excellent use of primary archaeo-logical evidence to bring it to life. During a visit, children pretend to be archaeologists, and discover how Mariotta's house was reconstructed by investigating some of the objects and structures which were found during excavations. Projected slides are ideal for use in school as they can be seen by a whole class at a time and make an excellent focus for discussion. By using slides children can travel to places which would not otherwise be possible and, in the same way as they would while looking at real buildings, find clues on the screen to life in the past. The use of slides during the project on Neolithic Scotland enabled children to compare the landscapes and monuments on Orkney with those in the North - East. If children are encouraged to look at and to question pictorial sources, and discuss possible interpretations it becomes easier for them to question written sources.

Considering the meaning of heritage

Archaeology provides a useful way of exploring heritage issues. Nowadays, many excavations, particularly in towns come about as rescue operations before a new road or shopping centre is built. Children can, through role play put themselves in the positions of developers, planners and conservationists, and discuss the ways in which decisions are made. A visit to the museum can stimulate discussion about the problems associated with the collection and ownership of objects. Children can also learn to look critically at how a building has been presented to the public and decide what measures have been taken to protect it for the future. Archaeology offers a tangible way for children to challenge what is currently considered to be our heritage, and to meet first hand some of the people who are employed to look after it for us. .

Understanding People in Place

Archaeology is by its very nature, spatial as well as chronological. By looking at history from an archaeological perspective, it is possible to combine elements of the key features of 'Understanding People and Place' with 'Understanding People in the Past'. Placing events in their geographical context often leads to a greater understanding of their significance. For example, it is no accident that Old Aberdeen grew up around St Machar's Cathedral. While the cathedral was being built it would have attracted hundreds of craftsmen and their families, who would have needed somewhere to live, food to eat, clothes to wear and entertainment.

All built and constructed features in the landscape are part of the archaeological record, whether a Second World War gun emplacement or a 6000 year-old burial cairn. Their location, choice of building materials and purpose were all deliberately chosen by people in the past. By using a series of historic maps, and carrying out fieldwork, it is possible to learn about the growth of a town or village, with true understanding. It is also possible to make more sense of monuments like stone circles, which are often located on rising ground overlooking what would have been fields nearly 5000 years ago, as places of celebration.

Conclusions

Children should be encouraged to understand that the study of the past can be a contentious activity. They need to be enabled to question a variety of sources of evidence, and make their own interpretation. Finding out about the past can be a rich and rewarding experience.

5-14: Opportunities and Obligations

Colin McAndrew

The most important point about the 5-14 National Guidelines is that the programme has created a comprehensive set of minimum entitlements for learners; and classroom teachers, whole schools, school boards, local authorities and external providers are required to respond professionally to fulfil these.

5-14 Programme for Curriculum and Assessment

We can trace the 5-14 Programme back to 1989 and the publication of a Consultation Paper on the Structure and Balance of the curriculum for primary schools and the first two years of secondary. The Education Minister at the Scottish Office was Michael Forsyth. The National Curriculum Council in England was rushing lemming-like towards implementation of a statutory, legally-enforceable National Curriculum. There was strong political pressure for (and from within) Scotland to follow suit. This was successfully resisted, although not the pressure for national testing. The Minister, reluctantly, accepted advice largely from the Scottish Consultative Council on the Curriculum (SCCC) , on the principle that 'if it ain't broke don't fix it'. Evidence had however been growing in the 80s, largely gathered by Her Majesty's Inspectorate (HMI) through the inspection process, that while many schools were doing well, there were deficiencies nationally in learning and teaching which ought to be addressed. Among these were the problems of transfer from primary to secondary (hence 5-14, a curriculum model unique in Europe, but now attracting attention and being adapted by systems elsewhere) the quality of experience for pupils in some curricular aspects, the overall curricular balance and a lack of a coherent system for assessing and reporting pupil progress.

Environmental Studies in particular was a target singled out by HMI for criticism.

For example, much work covered by Environmental Studies was in fact masquerading as such. A topic study of the *Vikings* could in the classroom be largely based on a fairly passive study of a work of children's fiction and death by 1,000 worksheets. There was little direct experience or active investigative learning. Little attempt was made to visit a relevant site to view or handle artefacts, or to investigate evidence such as placenames in the locality. Or the study was totally de-contextualised from the locality. Ideas of science and technology were generally absent. The same or very similar content was being offered in a P3 class or much later at P7, so progression in learning was difficult to uncover, if present at all. Children's pictures of Viking longships, sourced and copied from reference books, adorned the classroom walls. It was all pretty inadequate Environmental Studies, probably poor Art and definitely a bad way to treat children's literature.

The process of review and development began, and over a three-year period consultation documents were negotiated which then became National Guidelines. These organised the 5-14 curriculum into five broad areas of study, gave approximate time allocations to each of these, indicated the role of cross-curricular themes, and the picture was completed by the production of Guidelines on Assessment and Reporting procedures. Two important things must be stressed. The National Guidelines resulted from a review of identified good practice and they also describe pupil attainment as a series of minimum competencies at different stages. The 5-14 programme set out to provide a curriculum which is founded on coherence, continuity, progression breadth and balance. It is no secret that Environmental Studies was the most difficult area in which to secure some sort of consensus about how it should be organised and what it should contain.

5-14 Environmental Studies

With 5-14 Environmental Studies, for the first time in Scotland we now have a clear national statement which all schools are expected to take fully into account when planning this aspect of the curriculum. HM Inspectors will from now on look for evidence (in School Development Plans and through inspections) that schools are beginning a structured review of practice. Many things will not change, or should not, if schools have been gradually evolving and improving provision. However a review of practice highlights areas where action is required over time to meet the requirements in the Guidelines.

It would be wrong to isolate opportunities to incorporate the interests of archaeology into the curriculum in the domain of Environmental Studies alone. There must be sensory and affective opportunities also - not just a concentration on the cognitive domain. I think of the role of the Expressive Arts (such as Arts and Crafts, Drama, Music) in particular, also of contexts in many forms of Language work, and so on. But Environmental Studies can reasonably be viewed as the main 'carrier' with the others perhaps as contributors.

I commend three major aspects of the Guidelines as worthy of continually re-visiting and that should be the primary focus for curriculum planning rather than the detail of targets. These are:

- The statements of Attainment Outcomes, their various Components and Key Features
- The Strands of Knowledge, Skills and Attitudes
- The Broad Planning Stages of P1-P3, P4-P6 and P6-S2.

We in Scotland have a proud tradition of a thematic, cross-curricular approach to learning and teaching in primary schools. The National Guidelines acknowledge this but call now for greater rigour and selection. The role of distinct 'subjects' is recognised, particularly for S1-S2, but also towards the upper end of the primary school. However, in secondary schools the need for interdepartmental co-operation is stressed, otherwise content could overlap or important connections between subjects omitted. The already-devised structures (such as school clusters) and experiences of primary and secondary liaison (gained through English and Maths) will be very important to ensure progression (and equally an avoidance of duplication).

Concentration on one or two Attainment Outcomes only is suggested as the major focus for a topic or study, in the expectation that attention will be paid to the rest at other times in order to achieve balance and progression. A variety of approaches is also encouraged. For example in *Understanding People in the Past*, models such as lines of development (e.g., tracing developments in *Transport* through a chronological period) or patch studies (*Life in a Mediaeval Burgh*) are both appropriate, and the topic may also emphasise some aspects of say *Health Education* or *Technology*.

Criteria for selecting content and methodology will include considerations of how to promote first-hand, active, investigative learning situations, to develop fieldwork skills, to include a local and Scottish dimension, how the topic will be resourced and a plan for the roles of the remaining Strands of:

- Collecting Evidence
- Recording and Presenting
- Interpreting and Evaluating
- Developing Informed Attitudes.

The three-year cycles of P1-P3, P4-P6 and P7-S2 are promoted as the way forward for collaborative planning and as a way to ensure that progression is catered for. The planning cycles are useful for resource providers in targeting resources - matching contexts and content to pupils' attainment, relating their previous experience and deciding at what stage it is appropriate to introduce particular ideas.

The National Role of the SCCC

The Scottish Consultative Council on the Curriculum (SCCC) is the principal advisory body to the Secretary of State for Scotland on all matters relating to the curriculum for young people aged 3-18. The SCCC provides guidance and support in the form of Exemplification Materials, Staff Development Packs etc. Our *Values in Education* statements offer a set of general principles which are a useful context for schools looking for a starting point to review present practice in Environmental Studies. These statements emphasise the importance of developing a sense of belonging, a sense of self esteem, a respect for others, a sense of social responsibility and a respect for learning.

The SCCC's role then is mainly in policy development in the curriculum. Education Authorities are locally responsible for school education and many produce their own guidance and support materials, sometimes in collaboration with other partners. SCCC is keen to support meetings to listen to the priorities and concerns of teachers, trainers and providers. Where are the problems, the opportunities and the gaps? What services could we usefully develop further?

A range of 'Products' has already been developed by SCCC: The *Environmental Studies 5-14 Staff Development Support* pack should be a useful reference for archaeologists wishing to be involved in school education. It contains seven books which include material on Early People, Village Study and Fieldwork. This pack is:
- based on good practice - and widely trialled and evaluated,
- customised to 5-14 in a way which has been well-received and which teachers find helpful,
- based on consultation with relevant experts and partnerships, including archaeologists, field study experts and historians where appropriate; and

- reinforces the topic-based approach in primary schools.

It contains advice on planning - including assessment, differentiation and fieldwork. A Fieldwork Guide was seen as necessary to stress the need for advance planning and effective follow-up, teaching and learning practicalities, and advice on how to make the most effective use of visits.

The topics selected are not prescriptive. As exemplars they are meant to offer transferability (or the ideas behind them) to different localities and to related topics. Note the stress on *staff development*, rather than pupil materials - although there are suggestions for pupil activities - resources to support activities are probably already available or are being developed elsewhere. And we believe that the teacher has the autonomous right to plan and deliver at that level.

Conclusion: the role of providers

In recent years providers have undergone many changes - proving that museums are stimulating, fun places - not simply the residences of stuffed birds. You have done a tremendous job and I'm sure you will continue to do so. It is not my place to suggest where you should be going now and I only offer a few thoughts from a personal perspective.
- Work on public understanding - as science has successfully done - and use the media to promote your activities.
- Use a *Scottish Strategy for Environmental Education* as a reference point for future actions
- The new unitary authorities offer a challenge which must be faced - target councillors.
- Develop your role in pre- and in-service training - skilling the mass of teachers is the key.
- Consequently, consider carefully the production of 'another bloody pack' (of course there is always a need for new materials, but caution, and quality is the big issue, and not just paper-based products).

- Collaborate with other providers. (Regional Environmental Education Forums as a mechanism? Or a model?)
- Seek partnership initiatives as cost effective.
- Always keep teachers involved in the process.

Much of what I have said is to do with the processes of change and the management of change. People are often hostile to the notion of change because of the personal responses they will have to make. But History is the story of change. Without offering children stimulating ways to gain an understanding of the Past I don't see how they can relate to the Present, never mind considerations of what sort of Future they will opt to contribute to. It's all part of this thing we call 'Environment' and our collective aim should be do a little better than our forebears.

Interpreting the Landscape

Investigating Loanhead of Daviot stone circle

Education in the Middle of Nowhere?

Peter Dreghorn

Glenochar Fermtoun and Bastle house lie over 1000 feet up on the borders of Dumfries and Galloway Region and Lanarkshire. It is remarkable that several families lived in this windswept and isolated place 300 years ago, bearing witness to the hardy folk of the time. The site was discovered 8 years ago and the Lanarkshire and District Archaeological Society excavated over that period. Now restoration of the site is taking place and at the same time a series of school visits using an educational pack produced by our Development Service in conjunction with local schools and Biggar Museum.

Glenochar Bastle House

As an amateur archaeologist and professional educationalist, I saw that the site had just enough extant stonework and structures to give clues to young people as to the origin and life-style of 16th Century Scotland. It also struck me that the strands of the new Environmental Studies curriculum mirror the work of archaeologists who have to plan, collect evidence, record, present and interpret the results. They also have

to develop informed attitudes and a knowledge and understanding of the period. The pack was therefore designed to enable the children to actually practice archaeology.

One of the activities is a simulated 'dig' in the classroom. This emphasises the need to leave the site undisturbed and to develop a respect for the real and replica artefacts. Each artefact is carefully trowelled from a sandpit and its attributes, such as the feel, colour, size, shape and possible use, are recorded on a chart. Some are easy to identify - a key is a key! However, artefacts like the spindle-whorl lead to more discussion and children are discouraged from concluding and naming the article until all possible attributes and notions have been discussed. Some articles, such as a clay pipe, provide a clue which can be used later in the project. When they discover that hundreds of similar pipes were found on site and when they also learn of the price of tobacco at the time, the children can make an interpretation of the relative wealth of the people. The 'dig' is the lynch pin of the project because it stimulates the imagination and curiosity of the children who then become interested in planning the site visit with the aid of maps and photographs. In the past, teachers may have planned site visits without involving the children; now they are required to develop the children's own planning skills and even to encourage them to decide on some investigative activities themselves.

On site, the children split up into groups and focus on one building rather than covering the whole toun. They measure, sketch and record what they see, making a first informal interpretation. One restraining force to site visiting is the weather - Glenochar has horizontal rain for most days in the year which is not conducive to clipboard activities, alternative methods of recording which don't involve grappling with a sodden paper in the rain such as video and tape recorder have proved popular!

Back at school the results are presented to each other in the form of displays, role play and talks. Even if erroneous, the children's suppositions are accepted since they are based on real scientific evidence that they have recorded. Later on they may rethink that notion after the museum visit. All through the project the children keep their own records of their work and contribute to major displays and talks when necessary.

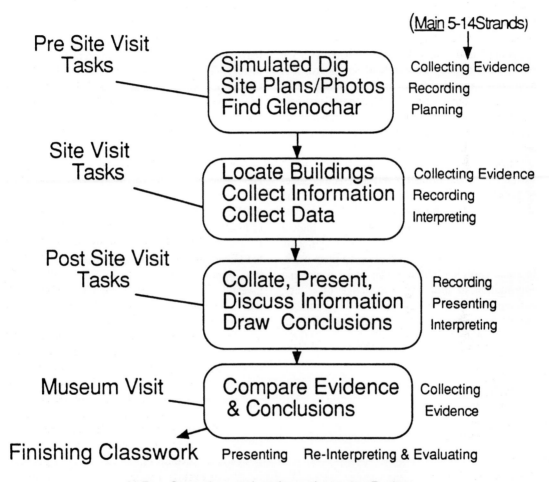

Glenochar Archaeology Project suggested pathway

Having planned the visit, worked on the site and had initial discussions, they plan a museum visit. Again, tasks are given to the children which help them revisit the things they may have looked at on a map, photographs and on site. This is a very intense activity and very different from the usual museum worksheets given to children. Here they are actually having many of their own theories confirmed or challenged and their involvement is total - cries of 'So that's what the slates are for, I thought there would be a slate roof!' and 'It looks really snug in the loft of the Bastle when you see the wood and sheep wool around' are heard. It is well known that if children are given things to do in a context and activities which build up their natural investigative techniques then the knowledge and understanding is deep and remains in the unconscious.

At the end of the project a self-assessment sheet is used which asks the children to reflect on the skills they did or did not use, such as using the equipment correctly and recording in a logical manner. Finally, a 'Young Archaeologists Certificate' is given in recognition of their work. In some cases the children can make a genuine contribution to the local knowledge of a site, looking at it with uncluttered and unprejudiced minds. At the very least they will know how to interpret a collection of stones and the importance it has in our heritage which to the layman represents....... a collection of stones.

Teachers who have used the pack have needed support, not in actually doing the tasks, but in developing the courage to go forth and investigate a site about which they have almost no knowledge. As children, the teachers would have been educated at a time when the interpretation of history was done for them leaving them with a set of apparent truths about history. This has been challenged by the 5-14 Guidelines which emphasise that the acquisition of knowledge is only one strand of Environmental Studies; the main emphasis is on the development of skills which the children apply to their work.

Her Majesty's Inspectorate are very critical of some topic approaches in school which emphasise the language and imaginative aspects of history and are often too general such as 'Let's Do the Romans this term.' Site investigations like the Glenochar Archaeology Project offer schools the opportunity to carry out a historical investigation on a well-focused topic by doing real archaeology and so covering the requirements for the curriculum.

Why 'How to be a Detective'

Val Turner

The concept of having a Shetland text book about archaeology originated in the Education Department of Shetland Islands Council. As far back as 1979 the Education Committee had felt that there was a need for resource materials on local themes to be produced for primary school pupils. Three books appeared as a result: *Footprints* written by JW Irvine, a former head teacher, dealt with Shetland's history during the last 100 years; *Shetland Animal Studies* produced by Rod Thorne, who taught in several of the country single teacher primary schools, which was to incorporate the most recent concepts about teaching environmental studies; and *Jarm and Jeemsie* which was a translation of a German poem into Shetland dialect by language teacher Derrick Herning. About four years after this last appeared, the committee approached a variety of people to write further volumes for the series. None of these were teachers and there was no fee available, so most of the proposed volumes foundered. Shetland Amenity Trust, however, agreed that I, as Shetland Archaeologist, could legitimately do this within the remit of my job.

By the time I was asked to write a book, I had been in post for two or three years, and was increasingly being asked by teachers to go into schools. Having no teacher training behind me I felt very inadequate. Desperate pleas to archaeological colleagues for help, and in particular to English Heritage who had been running courses for teachers about archaeology - but not vice versa, fell largely unheeded. Meetings of like-minded colleagues at Institute of Field Archaeologists conferences where we would pool ideas were very valuable, and eventually I spent a highly informative morning with educationalists from the Ironbridge Gorge Museum, as part of the Heritage Management course. I continue, however, to feel that learning on the job is far from ideal.

I had decided from the beginning never to go into a classroom in order to provide an afternoon's entertainment - the class had to be working on a theme which archaeology could slot into. I have regularly slotted into Viking themes, but also into projects as diverse as 'Homes' and 'Religion'. When the idea of the book was suggested, I admit that I saw it as a glorious way of avoiding ever having to go into a classroom again - I would put all my ideas in writing for teachers to use for themselves! Of course, once the book became available, I was invited just as often, if not more.

The Education Department set up a committee of teachers with an interest in archaeology to help and advise me as the book progressed. When we met they were always very enthusiastic, although they did not have a clear idea of what they wanted as an end product.

The difference between history and archaeology

On beginning the book, I sat down to write the type of book which I had wanted and found it did not exist when I was a youngster: a basic and readily intelligible introduction to archaeology. (I had decided by the age of 10 or 11 that I wanted to dig up bones when I grew up!).

The book evolved into four sections. Each contains activities or games and ideas for the teacher to use, and as one teacher pointed out to me, it would take an entire term to try everything out! The first section, *"Finding the Evidence"*, looks at what archaeology is and takes the reader through the various methods by which archaeologists find out about the past. *"Archaeology is the study of the past by looking at people's rubbish..."* The examples used are all from Shetland, and the types of monument are all types commonly found in Shetland, but the introduction to techniques is one which could be applied anywhere in Britain. *"Geophysical survey is a process used by archaeologists to find out what is under the ground without removing any earth..."* Local types of sites could easily be substituted by the teacher.

The second section, *"Putting the Evidence Together"*, consists of a chronological description of the types of sites to be found in Shetland and includes places to visit in every island: it serves the purpose of a gazetteer, planned to hold the interests of every young visitor. *"There is another broch site in Cullingsburgh, in a rather strange place. Can you find it?..."* The section ends with thoughts about experimental archaeology - and activities which children could undertake under supervision. *"When archaeologists think that they know how things worked in the past, they can sometimes put this to the test..."*

Part three I called *"Iron Age Space and Viking Invaders"*. The intention of this chapter was to present evidence and let the children make up their own minds about what really happened when the Vikings came to Shetland. *"So now you have thought about the different kinds of information which we have for the Viking age in Shetland. This is the evidence which the archaeologist-detectives can find... What do you think?"*

Iron Age space and Viking invaders

The fourth part consists of activities built around a visit to Shetland's internationally important site, Jarlshof. This is site specific, but again, adaptable to other sites. Some schools have used this chapter as part of a project, and on two occasions I have accompanied groups of children carrying out part of the project to the site.

I acquired illustrations from a wide variety of sources. I drew my own maps and one of the teachers on the committee, Jill Blackadder, drew some reconstruction drawings for me, and Sarah Cummings drew a few cartoons. Wishing to develop the illustrative aspect of the book further, I found an article in an archaeological magazine which contained cartoons by Chris Unwin. I knew immediately that she was the cartoonist whose touch was required. I spent days phoning all over Britain trying to track her down, at the outset not even knowing if I was looking for a man or a woman! Astoundingly, my hunt coincided with her husband (an Inspector with Historic Scotland) being on what was perhaps his only visit to Shetland, and my puzzle was solved in a Lerwick pub. My approach was then to send Chris selected paragraphs and phrases and to ask her to illustrate them. She also undertook a few reconstruction drawings as well. And so, after months of hard work, *How to be a Detective"* was born.

The print run of 1000 copies was distributed around the primary schools of Shetland but an increasing number of people asked about the possibilities of obtaining a copy for themselves. I was lucky because a local sponsor came forward unsolicited and offered to invest in a publicly available edition, and so, with some revisions to take account of a non Shetland readership, the book was reprinted.

A human tape measure

When I am asked into schools these days, the children have usually already looked at my book, but the teachers usually leave the activities up to me. I am always amazed by the amount which the children have picked up before I arrive. It also serves to make the children even more excited - not only are they getting an archaeologist to visit, but an author too! (As one child said to his teacher after my visit, "Now I've met two famous people: Cliff Richard and Val Turner"!!)

The way I use the book varies enormously, depending on the needs of the teacher. Being Shetland, it is only in the Lerwick schools that there are single year classes. In some places, one class contains the entire school. At Hamnavoe Primary School we tried burnt mound cooking with the older children. The class successfully cooked turnips, potatoes and eggs, and since we were on the beach, some of the shellfish were pulled off the rocks and thrown in as well. It was

one of the more dangerous activities in the book though, and I was glad that the only accident was that the teacher melted the edge of her shoe. The same class also went to look at some fairly ordinary (for Shetland) archaeological remains near the school. These were included in a school trail as part of an environmental science project, as well as being candidates for maths lessons etc. On other occasions I have taken classes to Guardianship sites - Jarlshof, Mousa, Clickhimin and Stanydale have all featured at different times. Shetland is probably the only place where children would be taken for a walk of half a mile, across the moors, in a force 7 gale! Not that I would take children anywhere without a teacher and sufficient adult help. The same rule also applies to being in the classroom - I never do it without the teacher being on hand.

And the next project?... I have recently become involved with a local telecroft who wish to make a CD-ROM about archaeology in Shetland, based on the book. So, watch this space...

How to be a Detective is currently available direct from Val Turner, Easthouse, South Whiteness, Shetland at a cost of £7.50. ISBN: 0 9521158-0-8 Your local bookseller can also order it for you.

Historic Scotland Education Service

Marion Fry

Throughout Scotland there are over 300 properties in the care of Historic Scotland including prehistoric sites, castles, abbeys, industrial buildings, a black house and even a lighthouse. About 70,000 school children visit these properties each year under the Free Educational Visits Scheme and there are many more who visit as part of a family group.

One of the main tasks of Historic Scotland's Education Officer is to liaise with teachers and educational advisers to provide information and ideas for activities at properties in care. The aim is to make the visit not only enjoyable but also stimulating and educational. There are now over 16 School Packs providing visual material, historical background and activity sheets based on the 5-14 curricular guidelines which teachers can adapt to suit the needs of their pupils. In addition, there are also 12 Site Profiles providing an introduction to the site, curricular links and ideas for activities. 4 Drama Packs provide ideas for drama activities. Further site-based resources are being developed each year.

Direct contact with teachers is vital and receptions are held at properties throughout Scotland in April, May and September for both local teachers and students at colleges of education. These meetings have provided useful feedback on the education service and, in some cases, have led to the development of other educational facilities extending beyond School Packs. It is important that teachers have an opportunity to see what is on offer and to assess the value of a visit for themselves. The teachers who are most likely to make use of the facility must be involved as much as possible.

As well as site-based materials, there is also the wider-ranging 'Understanding People in the Past: A Teacher's Guide to Historic Scotland Properties'. Written by Sydney Wood, with contributions from Historic Scotland staff, this book looks at different types of sites in the care of Historic Scotland and shows the learning and teaching opportunities that they provide. Different approaches are outlined in case studies which are applicable to other sites and historic buildings whether or not they are in the care of Historic Scotland.

Stirling Castle kitchens from the school pack

In 1997, we are looking forward to the publication of a School Pack on Skara Brae which has been written by a team of teachers in Orkney in conjunction with Historic Scotland's Education Officer. It is hoped that the pack, with separate sections for teachers of Primary and Secondary pupils, will be of interest to teachers throughout Scotland. As well as providing slides, line drawings and information on Skara Brae, the pack emphasises the different approaches which can be taken when pupils of different ages and abilities study the same archaeological resource. There are also plans for two more guides for teachers : one which looks at using school buildings and another which highlights the value of Burgh Surveys which have been produced for a number of towns throughout Scotland.

Historic Scotland is keen to encourage schools to develop close links with monuments. In August 1996, pupils from Melrose Grammar Primary School were able to follow developments during an archaeological excavation at Melrose Abbey. As well as receiving daily information bulletins from the archaeologists (Kirkdale Archaeology) they made several site visits where they were able to ask questions, examine artefacts and take part in a number of activities. The pupils were extremely enthusiastic and their levels of understanding and interest increased dramatically over the fortnight. This is definitely an approach which we would like to encourage.

Of much longer standing is the link between Linlithgow Primary School and Linlithgow Palace. Here pupils in the Primary 7 class, in period costume, take pupils from visiting schools on a tour of the Palace. For many pupils the link is maintained when they move into secondary school for they become volunteer guides at the weekends and during school holidays.

Stanley Primary School has recently decided to develop its interest in the mills at Stanley. Over the next few years, the pupils at the school will be keeping a record of developments at the site and will be interviewing local people who worked at the mills. Their work will contribute to an exhibition which is planned for the official opening of the mills to the public.

In May 1996, over 1,000 school children took part in a special education event at Stirling Castle organised by the education service and run by Mrs Cooke of Cooke's Conundrums. Based in the new school room at the castle, the children were able to dress up in medieval costumes and either learn a medieval dance or try out medieval games. A highlight of the day was the opportunity to 'perform' in the Queen Anne Gardens or in the Palace itself. The event was so successful that we hope it will become an annual occurrence.

Outwith formal education; children's guides and quizzes are now available at a number of properties and Historic Scotland is also supporting the Young Archaeologists' Network which is being co-ordinated by the CSA.

The main aims of Historic Scotland are to protect Scotland's built heritage for future generations and to promote its understanding and enjoyment. By providing interesting activities for children and relevant information for teachers, the education service is contributing towards achieving that aim.

For further information about sites and resources, please contact Mrs Marion Fry, Education Officer, Historic Scotland, Longmore House, Salisbury Place, Edinburgh. EH9 1SH. (0131 668 8732)

Looking for Clues about the Past with Aberdeen Urban Studies Centre

Allan Paterson

The Centre is an urban environmental education resource base which is part of Aberdeen City Council. Formerly serving Grampian Region, we will continue to provide services to schools in North-East Scotland and beyond for the foreseeable future.

1. Skene Square School - A Victorian Interior

   Social Subjects: Understanding People in the Past.

   Studying people, events and societies of significance in the past.
   Developing an understanding of change and continuity, cause and effect, time and historical sequence, the nature of historical evidence.

The internal features of the school could be investigated further eg

Ceiling height

Victorians liked rooms to be airy. Today, awareness of the amount of energy needed to heat rooms with high ceilings has led to modern buildings with much lower ceiling heights and double glazed windows. (Ceilings have been lowered and windows double glazed in Skene Square School.)

Energy Conservation

Discuss why this is necessary. Investigate the energy conservation measures in your school. Could they be improved?

Heating

Information about how rooms were heated is contained in Aberdeen School Log Books, produced by AUSC.

Interior Decoration and Materials

Decoration in schools today is much brighter than in Victorian times. Investigate the technology that has enabled this to happen. Look at the materials used in the interior of your school. Compare modern synthetic compounds such as plastic and vinyl with natural materials used during Victorian times.

© Aberdeen Urban Studies Centre

Extract from 'Victorian Aberdeen' overview

We are primarily concerned with increasing individuals' awareness of the environment they live in, beginning with the local environment. The Centre has devised material that leads pupils into the environment to gain an understanding of the issues that affect it. A.U.S.C. has resources covering many different aspects of environmental education but I will concentrate on programmes with a historical focus and in particular those concerning the Victorian period.

To facilitate this learning process, pupils should be introduced to their environment at the earliest possible age. Indeed, pupils often know a great deal about their environment and this knowledge can provide an appropriate context for a historical study.

The Centre has looked at local resources which are available to help teachers fulfil the requirements of the 5-14 and Standard Grade curriculum documents. The units I will describe form part of an integrated, structured programme of work on aspects of Victorian life. These units, organised in 2-hour time slots, provide pupils with a variety of learning experience that give a stimulus to further investigations back at school.

Planning a programme of work

Many teachers in North-East Scotland integrate the units we offer and regard them as an essential part of a structured work programme. The Centre has adopted the Overview as a method showing the key concepts to be taught, how these link with 5-14 curriculum documents and suggestions for follow-up work in the classroom. The Overview gives teachers the opportunity to choose which key concepts they wish their class, or particular group of pupils, to concentrate on. As each teaching unit usually lasts approximately 2 hours, time is usually at a premium.

Skene Square School

Go to the ground floor of the school.

1) Write V beside Victorian features.

NV beside features which are not Victorian.

NS beside those which you are not sure about.

doors		balustrade		linoleum floor covering	
door frames		wall clock		fire doors	
electric bell and alarm		brightly painted walls		radiator	
strip lights		large central well with roof windows		Greek Key pattern on glass of doors	

Extract from Victorian Aberdeen workbook   © Aberdeen Urban Studies Centre

Having chosen the programme, teachers arrange with the Centre when to bring their classes. Copies of our material for adult helpers/leaders are sent to the school well before the date of the visit. As the Centre's material concentrates on key ideas, we normally advise teachers to use what we offer fairly early in their programme of work.

Learning programmes
The Centre's programmes give pupils opportunities to learn through first hand experiences. I have chosen the Victorian period to demonstrate some examples of the learning methodologies we employ. When pupils arrive at the Centre they already have some knowledge about Victorian life and what they want to find out more about. There are a number of units for the teacher to choose from. Most classes use two of the following units to create a whole day's programme. These concentrate on a number of key places and ideas.

- A Victorian school building - interior and exterior
- Housing - The tenement and Victorian villa
- Places of worship
- Work places
- Exterior decoration on buildings
- Migration to Aberdeen from rural areas
- Public services e.g. lighting
- Travel within the city

Victorian Aberdeen trail

The trail booklets, devised by trained teachers in the Centre, encourage pupils to look for evidence that will lead to an understanding of Victorian life. After receiving a brief introduction to map reading, pupils leave with their leaders, in groups of no more than 11, to go out into the environment. A period of approximately 5 minutes is left between groups. This ensures that pupils can hear what is being said, have the opportunity to contribute to discussion and prevents overcrowding on the pavement.

The trail begins by looking at the interior of a Victorian school. Later, pupils make comparisons with their own school environment. Many teachers look at home life in Victorian times and compare similarities and differences between the experiences of rich and poor. Seeing where people lived provides a stimulus and gives direction to further research in the classroom. Notes given to leaders indicate how this can be taught.

Pupils commonly ask questions of their own, usually about the extent of the accommodation and other social amenities. The exteriors of buildings combined with information from primary source documents can provide some of the answers. Comparisons with how the more wealthy lived are made later. These key ideas about a particular time period are learned through direct observation in the local environment coupled with the use of primary source documents. Teaching materials used within the programmes have been designed to make this possible. For example, the plan of Skene Square School provides an insight into classroom accommodation levels and the segregation of boys and girls.

When learning in the environment pupils soon become aware that, in many cases, there can be more than one possible answer. For example, while observing the exterior of a Victorian tenement they try to work out how many flats are in the building. Incorrect responses are used to show how individuals think. Pupils should be able to give an account of how they arrived at

their answers to, in effect, explain their thinking process. In doing this an insight is gained into the reasoning of others.

At all stages close observation and discussion are encouraged. Later, pupils compare the tenement with a Victorian villa and again discuss life styles of upper and lower classes.

Learning from interiors

Pupils are given the opportunity to see the interior of a Victorian church. They investigate and gain an understanding of the design features and record these through words and drawings. It is also important to give pupils opportunities to express what they feel about the building through discussion.

Picture Search

Picture Search at Aberdeen Art Gallery provides pupils with the opportunity to learn from another primary source material - the paintings themselves. This unit gives pupils insights into entertainment, social conditions, working life and attitudes of the time

Here we begin with a short teaching session using one painting. 'Flood in the Highlands' which enables pupils to gain an understanding of certain aspects of Victorian life. This is accomplished through a question and answer session. Following on from this pupils, usually working in groups, answer questions designed to shed additional light on life during this period. All questions can be answered through direct observation. Later, pupils look at other paintings in the gallery's collection to apply their newly acquired skills.

Museum of Education (A.U.S.C.) -
the Victorian Classroom

Pupils are taught in a reconstructed Victorian classroom. They experience at first hand what it was like to be a child in Victorian times. Teachers, parents and pupils, dressed in appropriate costume, take part in the role-play. Lessons are taught in the methods of the time, giving pupils a real insight into Victorian education. All the material we devise provides a stimulus to learning. Although the format is highly structured, many questions are open-ended, inviting a wide variety of responses. Discussion is encouraged in small-group settings which provides pupils with a chance to contribute. As observation comes first, all pupils are eventually successful. The clues, being concrete, remain in pupils' minds and provide a well-founded reference point for the future. Most pupils now wish to find out more!

Marischal Museum

As well as the learning programmes provided by the Centre, classes are also able to take part in Marischal Museum's 'Victorians' object-handling workshop. During this workshop children are able to handle, investigate and record a variety of Victorian objects, from a number of contexts, including lighting, farming, policing and laundry. This close co-operation ensures that the widest range of options are made available to teachers.

Conclusions

It is unlikely that many of the teachers using the Centre's resources consider that they are 'doing archaeology'. However, the skills of observation and investigation of first-hand evidence that are developed are archaeological skills. By using these resources children are able to discover how people interpret evidence to understand the way in which their environment is created.

Back to the Future:
Education at Kilmartin House

Damion Willcock

Archaeology in context

A firm commitment to education has from the outset been the main aim of Kilmartin House, expressed by fostering in children a sense of responsibility toward the local landscape. So how is it done? The commitment was realised a full year ahead of the opening by implementing a programme of education. As a centre for archaeology and landscape interpretation, this programme takes archaeology in its wider context; an approach which concords with the intention of 5-14 Environmental Studies to embrace all the social, physical and cultural conditions influencing the lives of people. The Kilmartin Glen still vividly demonstrates so many of the features which suggest its attraction and significance to successions of ancient people: rocky shores with pools of limpets and mussels, much the same as they might have been when Mesolithic people cast their waste shells in the still visible midden piles; fertile valley floors, and plugs of rock with commanding views. The marriage of the Kilmartin archaeology to its natural environment is reflected by the centre's two sources of public funds; Scottish Natural Heritage, the main funder, and Historic Scotland.

The education work is not limited to local schools; nor is it limited to archaeology. Other audiences include London school parties staying at a nearby residential centre, and schools nation-wide connected to the educational area within the Internet. The importance of informal education is also recognised with the establishment of a new environmental club for local children, attracting good numbers. The intention is to present archaeology within a context of education in the environment. A circling buzzard or the glimpse of a weasel wouldn't be passed over when taking in the ancient stones; after all the builders of those monuments would have witnessed the same creatures.

Learning *in* this environment is fun and must surely be a constructive way of learning *for* the environment. The museums programme of experimental archaeology - *Practically Mesolithic* - is just that. Funded partly by the Scottish Museum Council's Environment Initiative, the programme explores the skills of people who lived in the past, in the context of the landscape in which they lived. Events capitalise on the skills of craftspeople helping to augment the museum's collection. The main event to date has been the construction of a large six person coracle, everyday transport 7000 years ago. Local children had the opportunity to touch and smell lanolin, raw hide, horse hair rope and to cut willow to make their own miniature version of a coracle in what was the first experience of its kind for many adults too.

Discovery

The ideas behind simulated digs and hands-on experiences are described elsewhere in this book - they are, quite simply, inspirational ways of learning about archaeology, for any age. We have made a portable simulated dig, on the hunter-gatherer theme, which is available to local schools (I am sure that local antiquarians are also itching to have a go). The emphasis can be placed as much on other living things and the processes of life as on people in the past. Among the finds are seal bones, burnt hazelnut shells, a shell necklace and a bone flute made from a swan's wing - and yes, they can play it. A skills-based approach is well served by the simulated dig. It provides opportunities for selecting relevant tools to excavate, sorting finds into categories, recording the evidence that is uncovered, identifying explanations for the position or state of their finds.

The contents of the dig are complemented by objects which would not have survived the millennia but must have been used by Argyll's Stone Age communities: birch bark containers, animal skins and wooden shafts for the mounting of flint points. An accompanying teacher's guide develops the artefacts into project material. A piece of wolf skin provides the starting point for investigating living things which have gone from Scotland, and some, like the Osprey, which are returning with our help. Copies of these discovery kits are to be available from resource centres so that as many Argyll schools as possible will have access to them. A loan kit on the prehistoric theme is also planned.

An extension of the hands-on approach is to use the wealth of archaeological sites so close to the museum as a resource in themselves. We are fortunate in Kilmartin, being surrounded by the very archaeology which we wish to celebrate. A peek through the museum windows reveals one of the cairns of the Great Linear cemetery - a string of five enduring cairns built over a period of over a thousand years. Investigation of artefacts in the museum can be followed two minutes later by a walk to the monument in which they were found.

In the landscape

A nearby residential centre used by London schools is alive with new occupants each week of the year. We were pleased that they took up the offer of prehistory tours of Kilmartin Glen. Unimpressed faces are soon removed when an interactive element is introduced. To grasp an axe which was *really* used by someone from the Stone Age is high octane fuel to the imagination of an 11 year old. Enthusiasm peaks again when we storm the fort of Dunadd and look for the clues of wars and walls. Carvings of wild boar, and mysterious footprints set the scene as we anoint ourselves as Kings on the airy top, overshadowed by the distant Jura peaks. So what do children remember from such experiences? As far as factual knowledge is concerned, perhaps

little in the long term. Significantly, however, their investigative skills are challenged - and their imaginations are certainly stretched. If their enthusiasm was fired and they felt the past then I feel progress will have been made. As they say, "Its wicked, innit?"

Information Technology

Information technology is playing a significant role in the education service of the museum. Agenda 21, the blueprint for the sustainable future of life on earth that resulted from the United Nations Earth Summit in Rio de Janeiro in 1992, specifically addresses this potential. There is a need to strengthen, within five years, information exchange by enhancing technologies and capacities necessary to promote environmental education and public awareness. Every school in Argyll is connected by a local area network, Argyll Online, used mainly by teachers to exchange support materials and resources. For Kilmartin House, the network provides valuable access to Argyll schools. Messages can be sent to any individual school or sent to an 'All Establishments' notice board to which everyone has access. The notice board feature is particularly useful; for example a request for information on the topics whichteachers intend to cover in the term ahead can be sent to all schools with one touch of a button. There is also great potential for pupils themselves to use the network to contact the museums as part of their collecting evidence, as the geography of Argyll makes an actual museum visit difficult for many.

The museum has access to all those schools in Britain which subscribe to the BT CampusWorld system, the educational area with the Internet. A relatively small, but growing proportion of schools is connected, with over 3000 schools expected to do so during 1996. One of the first surveys to go on-line asked children to record their sightings of song thrushes. This was organised by the Young Ornithologists Club, the junior section of the RSPB which is one of the main providers of environmental education in Britain. This was the first time that material of this kind has gone on-line. Material provided by the Young Archaeologists Club is also planned. 5- 14 archaeology in the future could include accessing archive video footage, or 3D images of artefacts actually stored in the depths of some museum's vault. Now that's virtually archaeology.

Using Excavated Evidence

Primary school pupils visit 'Step into Medieval Aberdeen'

"Step into Medieval Aberdeen": Presenting Local Archaeology to Schoolchildren

Judith Stones

Archaeology in Aberdeen

Archaeology in the City of Aberdeen occupies a rare position within the framework of Scottish local government. The Archaeological 'Unit', as it is called, is situated within the Arts and Museums Section of the Arts and Recreation Department, and prior to April 1996 was one of only two *District* Council Archaeology Services in Scotland.

Over the period of some 20 years since the Unit was first established, its responsibilities within a broad local history context have considerably expanded, but the major objective remains the protection and recording of archaeology of all periods within the City District, and the presentation of results to the public at a variety of levels.

Aberdeen became a Scottish focus of excavation and interpretation of medieval urban archaeology because of a proven record of well-preserved remains of the medieval burgh beneath the modern city, and because of increased levels of city centre development in the wake of the oil boom of the 1970s.

In the 1990s, although opportunities for discovery through excavation remain, methods have been sought of exploiting the vast accumulation of data as a public resource. Excavation has taken place in many areas of the medieval burgh, in each case providing additional information about the burgh what the buildings - religious and secular - were like, what people wore, what they ate, what they looked like and what illnesses they suffered from.

Background

The *Step into Medieval Aberdeen* project was developed in the realisation that if we caught the enthusiasm of the young, they themselves would ensure in their elders an awareness of the importance of local archaeology.

It seemed prudent to 'locate' the project not only in time (the first decade of the 14th century) but also in space, and it was easy to select the area of the modern Bon Accord Shopping Centre, which was not only well known to most primary school children in the North-East of Scotland, but also, coincidentally, has produced some of the best 'domestic' archaeology of the medieval burgh. We concentrated on one particular excavation site, where the foundations of a number of post-and-wattle buildings, at least one of them a dwelling, were recovered, along with a vast array of evidence about their surroundings. Such material included the ditches and fences which divided properties behind the medieval street known as Upperkirkgate, an oven for baking bread, and pits dug into the ground for storage or rubbish disposal. Many of these site 'features' produced what archaeologists loosely call 'environmental' evidence: animal bones indicate the range of meat consumed by medieval Aberdonians , while soil samples taken in toilet or 'cess' pits provide unimpeachable evidence of diet in the form of fruit and vegetable seeds.

Also from around and within these 14th-century buildings has come evidence of the utensils which people used in daily life, often broken or discarded. Among examples are turned birch-wood bowls- in one case thrown away into a rubbish pit after it was accidentally put too near the fire- cooking pots, ceramic jugs and other tableware, spinning and weaving equipment, fragments of clothing and worn-out leather shoes.

A further range of artefacts, for which medieval Aberdeen is justly famous, is money, perhaps predictably in the form of coin hoards, buried in wooden, metal or ceramic vessels. Eight of these hoards, concealed in the early 14th century, have been found in modern times, and we were obviously anxious to weave them into the project storyline if at all possible.

The project itself

Although I suspect that it is advantageous to the children that their visit takes place within a working archaeological unit, there are also constraints imposed by that environment. We can only operate on the basis of one class per week, partly because of the disruption to our building and partly because that is all the time we can devote.

The class, which can range from Primary 3/4 to Primary 7, is divided into two groups on arrival, so that half the pupils can start their visit off as 'time travellers' and half as 'archaeologists'. The time travellers are guided along a very elementary form of 'tunnel', by a 'time controller' figure, actually Mairi Stewart, the drama teacher provided by the local education authority. She encourages them to look at 'windows' as they journey, in which they see the same Bon Accord Centre location altering as they move back through the centuries. At the year 1308 they stop, are told that they will be entering the 14th century, but cannot do so unless they are dressed in the manner of that time. Their guide leaves them to change (into simple costumes which can be worn over their ordinary clothes), and when ready they enter the yard and house of Mariotta Nicholson. She is an early 14th-century resident of Upperkirkgate, Aberdeen (in reality the same individual as the time controller, although by no means always recognised).

The 'reconstructed' house and yard, and their contents, are based as closely as possible upon elements excavated by us in the Bon Accord Centre area. However, the size and shape of the

house (there is only the interior and one exterior gable wall) are entirely controlled by the dimensions of the existing room in our building: and materials, although as authentic as possible, were greatly constrained by cost. Therefore we choose to see the reconstruction as a set within which the drama takes place, an aid to the creation of atmosphere, rather than anything approaching a museum representation.

Immediately upon entering the yard of Mariotta's house, the pupils are drawn into the brief drama, which takes no more than 20 minutes. Mariotta needs help to prepare a medicine for Robert the Bruce, currently lying low in the Strathbogie area. The pupils assist her, then hide the medicine (and a bag of coins) to prevent discovery by an agent of the Earl of Buchan, who is expected to visit the house. When the threatened visit takes place, the pupils have to 'cover their tracks' by undertaking a range of household tasks: these include shoemending, weaving, spinning, broom-making and pottery making. During these events, the children find themselves looking closely at the house and many of the artefacts within it.

While all this tense activity is taking place, the other half of the class is busily engaged in archaeology. After a brief introduction and 'training session' they undertake two tasks. They 'excavate' a small area, removing just one layer of soil to uncover (in painted plaster replica) part of a post-and-wattle house-wall and the reddened stones of a hearth or fireplace, recording the location of pottery and other objects which they encounter. They move on to identify and 'date' some similar objects (real medieval pottery, animal bones, metals and leather) using a 'reference collection' and a stratigraphic model to assist them. I, as an archaeologist, was initially very unenthusiastic about introducing any form of 'simulated digging', but was persuaded otherwise by the teachers whom we consulted at the outset. I still feel strongly, however, that this activity must always emphasise the role of excavation as one step on the way to constructing a broad picture of the past. There is otherwise a danger of reinforcing a public perception of

31

archaeologists grovelling in the ground, discovering 'interesting bits and pieces', labelling them and placing them on a shelf. In fact, of course, it is the next, interpretative, stage which really brings the past to life.

By the end of the morning, all the pupils have been both time travellers and archaeologists. At this stage, just before they leave, there is a short 'debriefing' and recollection session. They discuss what they found while digging, and draw their results on a big 'site plan'. Gradually they realise that in their 'excavations' they have found part of the wattle wall and part of the stone hearth of the very house which they visited during the drama, and that archaeology is in fact another way of travelling back in time.

It is very important that a visit to *Step into Medieval Aberdeen* is seen by teachers as part of a planned study topic (which may not be very obviously history or environmental studies, necessarily). To this end we provide a teacher's pack, which includes suggestions for class preparation and follow-up, and tries to relate a visit to the wider curriculum. For example the project can provide opportunities for development in language, expressive arts, numeracy and technology.

What do we think pupils derive from their visit?

So far the project has been received with enthusiasm by both pupils and their teachers/ helpers. It has been gratifying to us to see the amount of detail about Mariotta's environment which children seem to recall, quelling our fears that memories of the drama might predominate.

We hope to encourage children to look at objects from the past, for example in our comparatively static archaeology display at Provost Skene's House (the subject of a follow-up quiz in the teacher's pack) in a new light. We should also like to feel that visits to archaeological sites such as castles may have more meaning in the future.

I also feel that archaeology can appeal to people whatever their academic level. Some children

have shown enthusiasm about the use of mechanical excavators on site, for example, while others in the class derive interest from the minutiae of pottery typology or history. Indeed medieval archaeology itself has its own special application. It can be particularly appreciated by people whose existence is rooted in the urban environment. It utilises a wide range of different forms of evidence which it is the archaeologist's task to blend and meld: foundations of buildings of wood and stone, old maps, old documents, manuscript illustrations, skeletal material, seed and plant remains, all of which can be added to a comprehensive picture of the past.

From actuality to aspiration

It did not take us long to become aware of a demand for provision for the lower stages of local secondary schools, from where we have had have frequent requests for talks and visits. Originally we considered a similar, although more challenging arrangement for S1 and S2, centred upon a visit by them to us. Our naiveté soon became apparent when the strictures of secondary timetabling were pointed out to us. Clearly the answer was to provide a package which schools could use in the classroom. We dreamed of a 'Medieval Aberdeen Roadshow' and perhaps that will come about when we win the lottery, but as a beginning we are developing a video utilising CD-ROM Technology, backed up, before very long, we hope, by a handling kit, models, costumes, replica objects, and so on. The video, *Life in a Medieval Burgh - Aberdeen*, is expected to be completed by October 1996. It will include drama and archaeology, but unlike our Primary project it will exploit the evidence we have found at several different locations within the burgh, for example at the Carmelite Friary in the Green, at the harbour and waterfront and in Old Aberdeen. Pupils will be able to 'bring to life' the character of Mariotta Nicholson, early 14th-century resident of Upperkirkgate, through 'excavation' of her skeleton, then construct her surroundings by 'excavation' of her house and yard. They will then go on to add and visit other key elements of her 'town', examining, interpreting and where necessary calling upon other 'experts', to assist, until they have discovered as complete as possible image of Aberdeen in the medieval period. This is a bold venture, but an excellent challenge to archaeologists and historians trained to think theoretically and to gloss over gaps in knowledge. We have to know, for example, what a Carmelite friar might have done all day in the buildings we have excavated, think about the prevalent sounds of the medieval burgh and come to grips with the minutiae of buying and selling in the market in the time of Robert the Bruce.

What do we get out of it all?
This is where, at the very end, I have to declare entirely selfish motives. We want to 'educate' the planners, architects and councillors of the future to have a sensitive attitude to archaeology: what better way than to start when they are young?

Many years of experience have suggested that children are more prepared than some adults to work with us and to understand our attempts to preserve and interpret their past. And who knows? Perhaps en route we will have the chance to 'encourage' a few present-day developers, through their children.

Interpreting the Evidence:
Education from an Archaeological Unit Perspective

Adrian Cox

Introduction

The Perth-based Scottish Urban Archaeological Trust was founded in 1982 and is one of the longest established archaeological units in Scotland. Its primary purpose is to examine the origins, function and development of urban centres and their hinterlands, through excavation, fieldwork and research. In common with other archaeological units, the Trust endeavours to communicate the results of its work to the public and uses a variety of means to achieve this. This paper describes some of the methods we use at the Trust to educate the public about archaeology, often on a shoestring budget.

Over the last few years, the Trust has become more heavily reliant on developer funding for its fieldwork and post-excavation projects and has, like other units, to compete for archaeological contracts. Against that background, there have been no additional funds available to support the essential, or at the very least, highly desirable work of promoting archaeological work and making it accessible to the public. Undeterred by this, we have been able to maintain a small-scale educational programme and, when possible, to experiment with new approaches to presenting archaeology.

Educating adults

Much of this paper concentrates on educational outreach work with children, but it is very much in the interests of the profession to make archaeology more accessible to adult audiences as well. The Trust provides speakers from among its staff to address meetings of local societies, clubs and other organisations, occasionally during the day but more often in the evenings. A variety of topics or themes can be offered, ranging from current or recent fieldwork projects to talks about the archaeology of particular regions or towns, or on aspects of the Trust's post-excavation work, for example. Opportunities to speak to particular groups most often arise by the Trust being invited to provide a speaker, rather than being actively sought. However, the Trust organises a series of lectures on the archaeology of medieval Perthshire each winter, in conjunction with Dundee University's Extra-mural Studies Department. This is held in a different venue in Perthshire each year, in order to give people from different parts of the county an opportunity to attend.

Work with children

Since joining the Trust's staff in 1988, I have devoted the small amount of project time available and a fair amount of my own time, to getting an outreach programme for children up and running at the Trust. I have taken up this challenge with great enthusiasm, finding this type of work very valuable and rewarding. It seems to me to be a natural extension of post-excavation work, to communicate an enthusiasm for archaeology to a wider audience. My background before joining the Trust was not only in excavation and artefact research, two of my current roles, but also in supervising educational programmes, devising children's activities and organising site tours, open days and guided walks, for archaeological projects based mainly in the Midlands. Much of my educational work at the Trust is geared towards children of primary school age. Schools and museum education departments in both Tayside and Fife have been visited.

Using the evidence

One of the main types of activity we have been able to offer local schools is the classroom-based object handling session, accompanied by an illustrated introductory talk which provides a background to the archaeology and, generally, to the origins of archaeological finds and their uses as evidence. This latter concept is explained in a very general way, so as to whet the children's appetite for investigation and enquiry of their own, when presented with a range of different materials and artefacts. With the emphasis very much on active learning, the children are encouraged to ask their own questions of the objects and to gather evidence themselves. To help them, without imposing too much direction, an `object investigation sheet' is provided, offering some tips on how to search for evidence and providing a means of recording observations. Questions like `What was the object used for?', `Who used it?', `How long ago?' and `How did it find its way into its archaeological context?' can be addressed and discussed among the class.

Artefacts are also used to give the children an insight into what an archaeologist does. The children can develop theories about the objects, and then take this a little further and find ways of testing and defending their theories about objects through reasoning. These are skills which have uses beyond archaeology, and in practising these skills children can also have a lot of fun. Being an archaeological detective is fun, after all.

The children often become quite absorbed in examining and analysing artefacts and, as they learn more about the past through this direct encounter with its products, recognise that the past was peopled by individuals not unlike themselves, with similar needs and feelings. The exercise serves to bring the past within reach; whereas it might otherwise seem rather distant and abstract.

Use of animal bones (identified as to species by the Trust's Archaeozoologist Catherine Smith) in the handling sessions enables the investigation and discussion of the important role of animals in past economies. Modern society has perhaps become slightly unaccustomed to thinking of animals as sources of food and clothing, as well as material by-products such as bone, horn and antler. Nevertheless, children seem to be able to

take on this concept quite readily. Oddly enough, it is the adult audiences who sometimes find it more startling.

Handling sessions can be adapted to suit a teacher's particular requirements and to suit different venues and events. Although we have very limited resources at the Trust's offices in terms of space for children's activities, we can occasionally organise a kind of `roadshow' event outwith the classroom environment, for instance on National Archaeology Day. In these events I have been ably assisted by friends outwith the Trust, some of whom have experience of working with children in different settings.

Simulated excavations
Since 1989 I have introduced small-scale simulations of archaeological excavations into classroom-based workshops. To prepare for this activity, I build up layers and features (pits, ditches, walls, etc.) in miniature within a box, and a small group of children is given the task of excavating this miniature archaeological site.

This exercise aids an understanding of the *context* of archaeological objects. I am keen to put over the idea that archaeology is about people and about how those people lived, and not just about objects. Being able to investigate the simulated remains of buildings, rubbish pits, livestock pens and trackways, as well as the associated objects, the children can observe for themselves the types of associations used by archaeologists when integrating different types of evidence. They can also see how stratigraphy works. Another function of this exercise is to demonstrate the fragility of the remains being excavated. The children can observe, by experiment, that the more carefully they excavate, the more evidence will be revealed. Once again, recording of observations is encouraged, so a simple type of context record sheet and a finds record sheet are provided.

Given the limited size of the portable `site', this activity works best with groups of 6-10 children. The group can be split into a digging team and a finds team - teamwork promotes discussion and exchange of ideas - and the two teams can swap over at half-time.

Scale models and artist's reconstructions of town life in the past are immensely useful in stimulating the children's imaginations. A reconstruction is, of course, only a hypothesis, and questions always remain. I find it a useful exercise to discuss with the children the way in which all the different pieces of evidence have come together in the reconstruction, and to discuss the possible problems with the evidence, and alternative interpretations. In this way they can see that ideas about life in the past are not fixed, and that they can contribute reasoned interpretations of their own.

Craft workshops

Probably the best way of understanding how something is done is to try doing it oneself. Craft workshops, which can be classroom-based or based in a museum education department, for example, allow children to try their hand at making things, using some of the materials and technologies of the past. Pottery-making workshops have been organised, along with activity sessions in carding and spinning wool. These can both be adapted to replicate Prehistoric, Dark Age or Medieval technologies, and a link is also made with the present, in the form of more modern, machine-made pottery or textiles. The differences between pottery made by hand, thrown on a wheel or made by machine can then be observed.

Site tours and exploring the town

The Trust occasionally conducts an excavation in the centre of Perth, and an ongoing excavation, given the right conditions, can provide a valuable educational resource. Beside the excavation at 80-86 High Street in the Summer of 1992 a viewing platform was available, enabling site tours to be given to groups of adults and children. A small selection of finds from the excavation was displayed on the site in a secure case.

As part of Perth Partnership's tourist trail, the Trust has produced a series of information panels, based on the results of excavations and research, which are now located at sites of historical or archaeological interest around the town.

Some of my recent work with children has included giving a short, guided walk around the medieval core of Perth, as a follow-up to a classroom talk. The walk focuses on the form and geography of the medieval town, and sites of excavations are pointed out, with an explanation of the evidence gained from them. This idea can be refined with the provision of worksheets, so that observations can be made and recorded, and so that teachers can follow up the work in class. Also to assist in follow-up work, we can provide exhibition panels for classroom use, focusing on the archaeology of the town.

Work experience

The Trust is occasionally able to offer work experience placements to schoolchildren contemplating a career in archaeology. Children can gain first-hand experience of working on excavations and of working with archaeological materials. Pressures on staff time prevent us from being able to offer this more widely.

Publications

In 1984 the Trust published a booklet entitled 'Perth: the archaeology of the medieval town', which has been widely used by local schools. More recently, booklets on the local burial grounds at Greyfriars and Kinnoull have been produced, and a contribution was made to the popular publication on the archaeology of Dunfermline, 'The Capital in the Kingdom'. We would certainly like to produce further popular material.

Conclusions

It is recognised by a growing number of educationalists that archaeology's multi-thematic nature, involving studies of primary evidence, materials, technology and past environments, can make the subject an important part of school curriculum activities. In an archaeological unit such as the Trust, we have no large teaching collections or classroom facilities, but perhaps our most valuable resources are the archaeology itself and the knowledge and enthusiasm of the staff. As archaeologists we have an important role to play in educating the public about archaeology and the importance of safeguarding it.

I think that we will have achieved something very worthwhile if we are able to instil in the young people of Perth and elsewhere a deeper interest in, and appreciation of, their surroundings and their heritage.

Museum Education: We dig it!

Barbara Hamilton

Introduction

Mention that you are an archaeologist in company and a common reply would be, "Oh I always wanted to do that". So what is it about the subject that attracts people? As an ex-archaeologist, now working in the museum education field, I have dealt with many aspects of the profession, both field based and museum based.

The reality of the profession is not akin to the image that most media professionals would show. How many times have we seen an archaeologist in a white jacket, picking away at a skeleton or a nice piece of mosaic! Though this scenario can occur, who would really want to see the reality of muddy sites, rain and frost and wet drawing boards. Negative, but realistic.

So where does all that fit into real life? An excavation evolves as fieldwork takes place, post excavation work is carried out, reports are written, finds catalogued and stored. In most cases that would be the end, but in many museums there is now a second life for these objects in the form of public information or exhibitions for all, not just the expert. There is more than one way to display an object and there are more calls nowadays for some form of interaction with the object and public.

Background to the Education Service at Perth Museum and Art Gallery

Perth Museum and Art Gallery has an education section comprising one member of staff, who deals with education in its broadest terms. Within the walls of the museum this includes, wherever possible, ensuring exhibitions provide a 'hands on' experience for the visitor. Outside the museum there is a geographical area of over 2,000 square miles to be catered for.

There is a move in many museums to increase adult education, but I simply don't have the time. This is to some extent off-set by the work of curatorial colleagues in giving talks to local groups, e.g. Women's Rural, Probus clubs etc. The main thrust of the education service is towards schools, which demand 95% of the service effort. This follows a huge increase in school use of the service over the last 5 years which has benefited pupils with a more rounded and investigative learning experience.

When the final dark blue copy of the curriculum eventually reached us I decided that to maintain our audiences and to fulfil certain parts of the curriculum, I would write curriculum documents to fit all classes. The documents give teachers reassurance and a clear idea about what to expect and how the visit compliments their forward plan, as well as the project in general.

So what do we have?

We have available to schools in Perth and Kinross District a flexible selection of 20 classes. This includes history, natural sciences and art. All classes include cross-curricular work, with varying elements of craft, music, investigation, and handling sessions of natural sciences, history and art. To compliment the classes we have over 60 loan kits available covering the three main subject areas. As a further aspect we offer in-service training, sometimes specialist, sometimes more generally on the whole service, showing how the museum can resource and help teachers.

The service has been going now for about 12 years and in that time each successive Keeper of Education Service Services has brought their own new developments to the service. All have contributed to the increase in school usage already referred to. The demand is such that if teachers require to book a class they are advised to book 6 months in advance and the general waiting time has gone from 3 weeks to around about 4 months.

Its success is down to a number of factors. Teachers and pupils alike see the museum as a more approachable place. They have a name to contact for advice, and bookings. As time has gone by more of the collections have been put into use and where necessary replica objects have been acquired to enhance classes and loan kits. Word of mouth seems to have also helped. Often the museum service is mentioned at training days and head teacher meetings.

In-service training has helped to spread the word. The curriculum documents have been a great success and have been a good source of information for teachers completing forward plans. To keep everyone up to date with new developments a twice yearly news sheet is produced called the Musepaper. We also have an annual teachers' 'bash', at the museum involving wine, no children and a very welcoming atmosphere.

Archaeology and us

Perth Museum has extensive collections of archaeology, particularly from the medieval occupation of Perth (thanks largely to excellent preservation in the very wet soil). The collections also encompass social history, natural sciences and art, to reflect the rich history of Perth and Kinross District.

The straight subject of excavation is something that I am rarely asked for. This did however happen in 1991 when a teacher asked for a talk on archaeology to fit in with the topic 'Under our feet'. The class were 6-7 years old and even though I mentioned to the teacher that the technical side was a bit more in-depth, she had her mind set on it. I devised a simple excavation pit using sawdust and turned it into a quiz. Lots of time scales were covered using real artefacts, quiz sheets and replicas and all the children had a wonderful learning experience using most of their senses.

Despite a very positive evaluation sheet back from the teacher, to this day, I do not believe we covered practical archaeology. The learning outcome was to accept that certain things are not always possible in a museum environment, but you can try to adapt most requests to suit it. There was nothing stopping the teacher from going back to school and simulating the same exercise in the school grounds, hence having time to develop certain aspects maybe not covered in the museum visit. You can only hope that any advice you give for follow up work will be considered. Though often asked for a follow-up, the resources are rarely there to allow it.

The classes have been developed over the years. Ideas come from strange sources sometimes, whilst reading, shopping, drinking, communicating and innumerable other everyday activities. People in history did these things to survive, so ideas for new classes can stem from life. For example the realities of everyday life for the Romans can be communicated with herb samples; the Romans used herbs for cooking and medicine. This forms a useful contrast with visits to fort sites such as Ardoch and Inchtuthil where mock fights and raucous behaviour tend to be the order of the day. Work can also be carried out regarding cooking pots, recipes, medicine, warfare, living conditions, climate, clothing - the list goes on. It's amazing how much you can get from children by using a few pieces of pottery or simple finds, as long as you set the scene.

Another problem that I face is teachers asking for classes on subjects such as the Vikings and the Greeks. We don't have many objects covering either subject and it would be pointless trying to produce a class from so little. Therefore the variety of classes can depend on the availability of the collections.

Geographical restrictions

During the spring and summer I am the envy of the museum, loading up my car with my artefacts and driving off into the countryside. But in the winter it is obviously a different ball game. The furthest school is Glenlyon, averaging 8 children and a round trip of about 104 miles. You could question whether this is the best way to use the service, sending one person all that way to carry out a class for so few children. But when the service was first introduced it was decided to service the whole geographical area of the district. Perth and Kinross is largely rural in character with widely spread small communities. The transport costs for schools to come into Perth are prohibitive - Glenlyon school for example has managed two trips in but no more. They can sometimes rely on parents but most work and can't spare the time. Sometimes grants are made available to rural schools for visits to organisations such as museums. The curriculum guidelines suggest that schools use outside organisations as a stimulus to enhance projects but it doesn't suggest how schools fund this!

I am perfectly happy with the structure of our service, winter travelling and all. A museum should be a place accessible to all, whether this is in the museum environment or in an outreach capacity. Our funding comes from a grant from the Regional Education Department and money from the District Council. It is hoped that the changes in local government will not affect the service. The previous grant from the Region will be taken up by the new Education Department and the service will continue to grow and mature.

We could do with an assistant to cope with the growing demands on the service to meet client needs. Last year 186 classes were given, most of them taking up whole days. There isn't much point in travelling over 40 miles to stay for an hour and cram everything in. You also have to fit in with the school day. So if you arrive at 10.00 am you know that within 30-45 minutes there will be a break, which both adults and children need.

Conclusion
Due to the nature of the curriculum and that fact that most teachers do topics, as opposed to a straight forward archaeological look at a period in history, sometimes they may not feel that they are using archaeology. It is thought of as a practical subject in the field which produces finds. Many children and to a certain extent teachers will look on an object as being worth a lot of money - 'if it's old then it must be valuable, and archaeologists only find treasures'. Through museum education, allowing hands on, close contact with the objects we can show the objects in their most practical sense. Even though teachers may not see a box of medieval sherds as being worthwhile to his/her project on castles, through contact with a museum it can be brought to life with suggestions covering all aspects of the curriculum. The opportunities are endless and in Perth we are always willing to dig up new ideas and enhance the past.

"In Touch with the Past" and Glasgow Museums

Colleen Batey

Introduction

Most visitors to a museum have a view of the past - for some this is more accurate than for others, but it can nevertheless provide some kind of framework through which archaeological material can be interpreted. Static museum displays rarely add to this basic outline knowledge, but if the visitor can be given the opportunity to handle real objects as part of a tactile exhibition, there are much greater possibilities for education. This is obvious for visitors of all ages, but it is especially important for the blind or visually impaired visitor. For these people, a visit to a museum can often only be limited to the smells emitting from the café or the confusing noises in the echoing halls - objects behind glass cannot be accessed personally and, in too many cases, labels are too small for those with any degree of vision defect! However, when items can be on open display the experience of a visit to a museum can be transformed. This need not be only a wet-weather activity, it can be exciting, stimulating, and above all, it is open to everyone.

Glasgow Museums has a large collection of prehistoric stone artefacts, most particularly axes and flint tools. Making use of the large Reserve collection, about 50 objects were selected - ranging through flint waste, axe roughouts, complete polished axes, arrowheads to impressed ceramics - to form the exhibition *In Touch with the Past*. All items were either unstratified pieces or ones commonly replicated in our collections. The aim was to introduce various aspects of prehistoric technology through objects - making and using stone axes, flint tools, hunting skills and skin preparation as well as the creation of fire - to both visually impaired and sighted people.

Practical considerations

The brief for the display was made more challenging by the need to produce a portable construction which would form part of the Glasgow Museums/Royal Bank of Scotland touring programme, It needed to be sufficiently sturdy to survive frequent moves, yet light and practical in construction. Additionally the units needed to be designed to have the flexibility to suit venues with widely differing exhibition spaces: from the spaciousness of the Art Gallery and Museum at Kelvingrove in Glasgow , to the more limited spaces of Kirkintilloch and Ullapool. The overall design, of six interlocking hexagonal units provided a large area of secure, versatile and accessible display. All the objects are placed in shaped insets in plastazote, an easily carved extruded material which is softer than polystyrene. Available in a range of bright colours, plastazote is user friendly to visually impaired visitors because it feels warm and pliable, in contrast to the cold, hard stone objects. The additional bonus of using dedicated pockets within the plastazote for each item was that it was easier to monitor for security purposes. Information about the objects was provided in both large print and braille text along a continuous band around the interconnecting hexagonal units, which were also intended to be accessible to wheelchair users. The initial plan, as used in Glasgow was as in Figure 18, but other venues experimented with the plan to produce a more linear form, and in one case space limitations allowed access only from one side.

The large-print text and complementary braille information outline the main areas represented on a series of seven upright boards incorporating Minolta raised images of simple line drawings. In about 50 or so words each panel covers:

Introduction to Prehistoric Life (with a line drawing showing a simple stone drill), *The Forest Falls* (illustrated by a hafted stone axe), *A Wonderful Resource* (showing a flint nodule being worked), *The Tool Kit* (showing a hafted flint adze), *The Home* (a hammerstone and flint chisel). *A Dozen uses for a Dead Deer* (illustrated by a flint scraper) and *Hunter and Gatherer* (demonstrating a flint knife/scraper in use on bone). The text is available to take away as the flip side of the poster and a taped version was prepared for those visitors unable to read braille. One blind visitor however explained that the use of headphones cut out all the background noises - a seemingly valued part of the visitor experience.

The objects themselves were all original pieces, with the exception of resin casts made of two carved stone balls. The obvious rarity of such pieces made this a necessity, but casting them proved to have its problems - the weight could be achieved, but not the coldness associated with real stone, with resin remaining warmer to the touch. The other casts used were a flint core and adjoining flakes and interestingly it was the cast flakes which proved to be somewhat irresistible to sticky Glaswegian fingers!

Fortunately few ancient axes remain sharp enough to cut, although they could wound if necessary, but smaller flint tools need care in handling; great care had to be taken in the selection of these, the aim was for the tactile experience to be a positive one! The inclusion of deer and wolf skins enabled a contrasting element to touch, but the deer did suffer throughout from unseasonal moulting!

A 'nation-wide' tour
The exhibition formed part of the Royal Bank of Scotland touring programme at Glasgow Museums and was booked virtually solidly between September 1993 and June 1996. 16 venues hosted the exhibition, from Chertsey in the south of England to Dingwall in Ross and Cromarty.

Several of the venues arranged supplementary displays and activities to coincide with the exhibition: in Aberdeen a modern flint-knapper was employed to demonstrate his skills. Most museums used the exhibition in an educational role to introduce both visually impaired and sighted children to archaeology. In Ross and Cromarty for example, children (mostly sighted in this case) were introduced to a neolithic landscape and art work, quizzes and local site visits were included where possible. There were four venues in all in the Ross and Cromarty area and at Ullapool, where the space was more restricted, the relatively flexible nature of the construction enabled a different configuration. The curator informs me that they had many visitors who came to visit the exhibition and then went on to join the Friends of the Museum! The Tweeddale Museum Service produced related teaching packs and supplemented the display with their own material, transforming a separate room into a neolithic scene with five workstations. Work which was undertaken at this venue forms the basis of another paper in this volume; this formed part of a formal educational evaluation of the exhibition which was of great interest to those of us in Glasgow Museums who are hoping to produce further exhibitions on similar lines in the future.

Conclusion
Glasgow Museums had not attempted an exhibition of this nature before, although the path had been well-trodden by colleagues elsewhere. Each project has its own specific problems, some of which can be overcome (such as potential loss or damage of objects, positioning braille incorrectly -usually upside-down) and others of which are harder to control. Without a doubt the biggest head-ache was the nature of the construction; how to produce something strong enough to survive the trauma of constant repacking and re-assembly, yet be light enough to be handled. This was addressed but was never fully resolved, and although some museums have complained of the complexity and bulkiness of the construction, others have said they had no problems at all!

One major problem was ensuring that the maximum number of visitors would be able to access the information available. Very few blind people can read braille (somewhat less than 5%), but the uptake of the audio tapes was disappointing, probably because use of the earphones cut out all other noises of the venue. Most visually impaired visitors attended with sighted companions, but all enjoyed the chance to handle material. In Glasgow, visitors with profound disabilities, including no sight or hearing did engage with the objects, if the yelps of delight were anything to go by, although the archaeology was likely to be incidental to that visitor experience...

Despite the number of problems encountered in the preparation and production of this exhibition, its extensive loan programme has testified to the success of the idea. There have been many advantages to presenting this material to a usually disadvantaged group, and as Rachel Hunter of Tweeddale has pointed out to me, this approach certainly helps us to give access to our collections in a different more potentially stimulating way . In common with other institutions, Glasgow Museums now has a much greater awareness of the requirements of visitors who have any kind of disability. *In Touch with the Past* was an experiment and we are now trying to put into practice some of what has been learnt in this : it is a steep learning curve, but successful results are rewarding to all of those who embark on it!

Acknowledgments

Throughout the preparation of the exhibition, support in many forms was supplied through the Strathclyde Resource Centre for the Blind, with additional publicity through the talking newspaper service. Practical advice, particularly in safety matters, was supplied by colleagues in the Hunterian Museum, Glasgow University, whose award-winning touch exhibition was held in 1990. I am grateful to the Tweeddale Museums Service for the evaluation report which raised so many interesting points.

In Touch with the Past: Tweeddale Museum 1994

Rosemary Hannay

Tweeddale Museum is a small museum and gallery managed by the Scottish Borders Council, formerly Tweeddale District Council, and staffed by a Curator, an Exhibitions Officer and a Museum Assistant. In 1993 the staff introduced a schools' project which is run in the spring of each year and aims to offer each primary school in the catchment area an introduction to a collections based topic which has been integrated into the 5-14 schools curriculum. The development of these projects grew out of a relationship established over several years with some local teachers which led to the creation of school loan packs and eventually to increasing demands on staff time for visits and loan materials. It was decided that if the Museum staff took a more pro-active role we could steer the schools towards the strengths of our collections (no more requests for material on the Vikings), and tailor each project to the resources we knew were available.

In 1994 the staff organised the second schools project, *In Touch With The Past*. This project was built round a touring exhibition from Glasgow Museums which consisted of an archaeological exhibition designed to encourage the handling of appropriate archaeological material. Tweeddale Museum's own small archaeological collection provided material for investigative workstations. These workstations were built round the following themes :- shelter, food, tool making and hunting. Each work station was also designed so that its topic could be introduced at a variety of levels. This was to reflect the age range of the children who would be involved in the project which covered primaries 1 to 7, ages 5 to 12. The workstation on tool making for example covered very early technology with flint cores and flakes for handling and discussion, a bow drill for

experimenting and wood, microliths and resin for making your own tool. In addition with older pupils early metal working was examined, including the smelting of ores and the creation of high temperatures with very simple equipment. At each of the workstations a similar attempt was made to keep the contents flexible.

Once the outlines of the project had been established we introduced it to the local teachers at a teachers' evening. Although the project was scheduled to take place in the spring of 1994, the teachers' evening took place in the previous October. In our experience it is vital to contact schools well in advance of any planned event as teachers often decide on their years topic at the start of the school year. We had a good turn out at the teachers' evening and by the end of the evening over half the available sessions had been booked. During the course of the teachers' evening we outlined the content of each school visit, emphasising how the project fitted into the 5-14 curriculum requirements and stressing importance of linking the visit to classroom work. A prototype workstation was set up to demonstrate the methods which would be used to encourage hands-on investigation. Feedback from teachers at this stage was encouraged and certain aspects of the project still at the planning stage were amended to incorporate these views.

The teachers' evening was followed up with a teachers' pack which was sent out to each class teacher who booked a session. The pack outlined what to expect on the day, the contents of the workstations and ideas for pre-visit and follow-up activities. As a result of this preparatory work most classes arrived on the day well prepared for what was to follow.

The project ran for four weeks taking place each day from approximately 9.30 a.m. to 12 noon and from 12.45 p.m. to 3.00 p.m. During this period over 500 pupils came through the project. Younger pupils from primaries 1-3 spent half a day, while older pupils from primaries 4-7 spent a full day. On arrival each class took part in an introductory session involving games. In the skeleton game pupils had to guess what would be left of a human body in the ground after decomposition, while the bin game used the contents of a household bin to work out information about who lived in that home. Each of these games was used to encourage children to ask questions about evidence and what can and cannot be deduced from it. At this point the class was divided into smaller groups of about seven to eight pupils and each group went to a workstation accompanied by a group leader from the museum staff. This system left teachers free to observe their classes which was one of the aspects which they valued most. It was also extremely demanding on the museum staff. Depending on the size of the class on some occasions almost the entire staff were involved for almost a full day.

In addition to the workstations which took place in one of the galleries, another large gallery was given over to an imaginative recreation of a pre-historic landscape using a chickenwire and plaster cave, stuffed animals such as deer, boar and wolves, trees, a pond and a shelter made of larchpoles and animal skins. Within this setting the second part of each school visit took place, involving activities such as spinning, basket-weaving, potting and cave-painting. These sessions were led by craftspeople, many local but a few brought in from further afield. Information about such craftworkers is available from the Scottish Arts Council. The local Education Department also provided a drama teacher to lead sessions in which pupils acted out some of the activities they had examined at the workstations.

Several field trips were also undertaken with a couple of the older classes, primaries 6 and 7. These were complex to organise, involving Education Department transport, qualified drivers and the permission of landowners to take 15 to 20 pupils through their fields at lambing time. However all these problems were overcome and local archaeologist, Tam Ward, took these groups through the procedures for carrying out a site survey at the settlement at Dreva.

In the first week of the project several sessions were given over for the use of special needs groups, both adults and children. This was our first serious attempt to work with these groups and their carers so the beginnings of the sessions were quite tentative. However the carers who accompanied each group were extremely well briefed and these sessions were particularly well received. These groups concentrated on what the Guidelines call the Expressive Arts, including drama, potting and painting. In addition, special handling sessions were run for these groups using material from the collection such as stone axeheads and flint arrowheads. A group also came from the Royal Blind School in Edinburgh. Glasgow Museums' touring exhibition was specifically designed for the blind and included labelling in braille.

At the end of the class sessions a fairly detailed evaluation was carried out. Evaluation forms were sent out to all teachers who participated and to all the artists and craftworkers who were involved. These provided invaluable feedback for the museum staff which has already been fed into the 1995 schools' project. Due to restrictions on staff time only one follow-up visit was made to a participating school. During the course of this visit museum staff were able to see work being carried out in class and to discuss the value of the project in more detail with the teacher and pupils involved.

The overall cost of the project was £3,500 of which £1,400 came from the Tweeddale Museum budget. The remainder came from a variety of sources including the Scottish Museums Council, the Scottish Arts Council and Borders Regional Education Department. In addition, the Museum services of a neighbouring District Council made a contribution to the cost of the production of the Teachers' Pack as they also took the touring exhibition *In Touch With the Past*. In addition to these costs the amount of staff time devoted to the preparation and implementation of the project has was considerable One part time member of staff was delegated to work solely on this project from January onwards. The actual implementation of the project took place in April and for about five weeks almost all staff time was devoted to it. The museum's weekend attendant was drafted in to cover day to day activities like answering the phone and dealing with enquiries from the public. We secured the services of a volunteer through a placement from Scottish Natural Heritage and she proved extremely helpful. In addition a number of local enthusiasts volunteered for the occasional day and made a very useful contribution to the overall project as well as freeing staff to deal with other matters from time to time. Nonetheless the whole project was a tremendous commitment from the museum staff and we considered very carefully whether we could continue to offer quite such ambitious projects in the future. That we are continuing to do so shows the degree to which the response of the local school proves that our efforts are on the right track and are being appreciated.

The long term benefits of *In Touch with the Past* have included a School Loan Pack which is in almost continuous use. The Teachers Pack developed to accompany the project has been taken over by the Education Resource Centre of the Regional Council and is used throughout the region. In addition the project served to alert a wide range of educational staff from drama teachers to those dealing with special needs of the value of archaeological collections as a teaching resource and of the innovative ways in which museum staff can work with pupils within the 5-14 Guidelines.

Talking and Touching:
Archaeology and Education in Marischal Museum

Neil Curtis

Groups of children visiting Marischal Museum usually take part in one of a range of hands-on workshops, with topics ranging from 'Scottish Prehistory' and 'Ancient Egyptians' to 'Victorians', 'Inuit of the Arctic', 'Shape' and 'Materials'. While the first two of these topics are commonly thought of as being archaeological, few of the children or teachers taking part in the other workshops would consider that they were 'doing archaeology'. An archaeological approach, however, lies behind them all.

Archaeology and the curriculum

The 5-14 Curricular Guidelines do not mention 'Archaeology', nor even 'History' or 'Geography' as sub-divisions of Environmental Studies. Instead, the heading 'Understanding People in the Past', 'Understanding People and Place' and 'Understanding People in Society' are used. These are not merely cumbersome synonyms, but are an attempt to break down rigid subject boundaries and emphasise the value of different approaches to the study of people.

When trying to understand the lives of people in the past, it is not enough to rely on traditional political history or even the achievements of social history in emphasising the daily lives of ordinary people. Rather, these approaches need to be pulled together, along with the study of population change, technology, the impact of place and changing religious beliefs to understand long-term patterns of continuity and change. This has been demonstrated by the historian Fernand Braudel who emphasised the importance of the routine activities of daily life in maintaining and developing the long-term structures which underlay political history. An archaeological approach, with its use of material culture, the landscape, interest in long-term change and links to other disciplines, has a crucial role to play in developing an understanding of people in the past.

Archaeology is the best, indeed the only, approach to investigating the lives of people in the distant past before there were written records. People have been in Scotland for about 10,000 years, but there are written records for only the last 2000 years - and for much of that period they are often little more than lists of kings, treaties and battles. It is not, however, an approach which is restricted to prehistory. The lives of most ordinary people do not appear in historical records until the last couple of centuries, while many aspects of life that we now find interesting were not written about in the past. For example, survey and excavation of 19th Century buildings has helped to reveal the living conditions of people during the Highland Clearances and the industrialisation of Scotland, and even the study of Second World War coastal defences has revealed how people adapted War Office plans to suit local conditions. To get a full understanding of people in the past, therefore, it is essential to use an archaeological approach as well as historical approaches.

Another attraction of archaeology lies in the nature of its evidence. Few children investigating the Wars of Independence are able to see the real Declaration of Arbroath, let alone handle it. On the other hand, not only can they have the excitement of visiting castles of the period and handling broken pottery excavated from medieval houses, they are able to use this material for their own investigations. The 5-14 Guidelines emphasise the importance of using primary evidence, not just photographs or facsimile texts. Much of this evidence is now cared for by museums throughout the country, but it is important to remember that, apart from size, there is no real difference between the ruins which survive in the landscape and objects in museums. Indeed, the best archaeological investigations look at objects in their context. Was a pot found buried next to a skeleton or in a midden next to a house? The answers to these questions will have to consider the impact of both place and society on people's actions. This emphasises the role of archaeology in making links between the various aspects of Environmental Studies.

Archaeology in Marischal Museum

Marischal Museum's collections consist of thousands of objects which have been made or used by people in many different times and places. There is a wide range of objects including a flint chopper used in the Ice Age in France, 4000 year old beakers from burials in North-East Scotland, Ancient Egyptian wall paintings, 19th Century Aboriginal Australian head-dresses, medieval Scottish coins and a teddy bear bought in Union Street in 1990. In common with many museum collections, very few of these objects come from archaeological excavations; they are the gifts of graduates and friends of the University, reflecting the lives of their collectors as much as they do the people who originally made or used them.

As few people have had the chance to develop their skills of object investigation, most museum visitors rely on the labels beside objects which explain their provenance and their place in the exhibition. How much time do they spend looking at the objects compared to the time they spend reading the texts? Objects in glass cases are perhaps of little greater value than images in a book to children visiting the gallery. It was for this reason that the museum developed its series of object-handling workshops in which classes can handle, investigate and discuss objects of equal quality to those on display. We hope that this approach will enable them to develop their skills of object literacy.

The use of high quality authentic objects emphasises the importance that the museum gives to its work with schools, and offers greater scope for investigation than would be possible with replicas or second-rate objects. By discussing the potential damage that irreplaceable objects can suffer by careless handling, uncontrolled humidity and sweaty hands, children can learn to appreciate the privilege that object-handling brings. Indeed, the workshops have resulted in remarkably little damage to the objects that are used. It is also worth considering that, in the long term, an appreciative public may be of greater value in caring for collections than will restricting access in the short-term.

The workshops have been designed to link to topics that are popular in schools, though sometimes they offer the opportunity to widen the scope of the project. For example, classes in the North-East investigating the Vikings are encouraged to find out about the Picts who lived in the area at about the same time. Likewise, school projects on prehistory can often emphasise the primitive nature of technology in the past, but this can be contrasted with the beauty and complexity of some of the objects that the children handle. To help teachers to integrate their visit to the museum with work in the classroom, the workshops are available on demand throughout the year (as long as museum staff and space are available) and an information pack that outlines the workshops has been distributed to all schools in the North-East and is available free to teachers. This information is supported by a booklet, *Learning with Objects* which was written by Kim Davidson, a teacher seconded to the museum, and suggests ways in which working with objects of any age can contribute to many areas of the curriculum. It suggests activities for investigating objects under headings such as 'Looking at Objects', 'Asking Questions', 'Describing Objects', 'Classifying', 'Relating Structure to Purpose', 'Working from Fragments' and 'Establishing a Sense of Time'.

Developing archaeological skills

An important feature of archaeology is the links that it has with other disciplines, such as surveying, illustration, experimental reconstructions, radiocarbon dating, pollen analysis, aerial photography and even forensics. As well as offering insights into the lives of people in the past, archaeology can therefore contribute to developing the wide range of the skills that are demanded by the curriculum. Perhaps the most important skills are those which involve the critical use of evidence; asking questions, creating hypotheses, recognising the reasons for alternative views and so developing an informed opinion. Why do different people ask different questions? How do you judge between different interpretations? Knowledge about an object is created by an individual in their own way as they investigate an object: it is not something that is transferred from the expert to the novice.

An approach to the investigation of an object which depends on the continuous interaction between evidence and imagination is so much richer than an approach which merely gives a name and a date to an object. For example, an artificially shaped piece of sandstone with the shape of an axe carved into one face can be classified as a 'Bronze Age axe mould' or can be the focus of an imaginative narrative that includes the story of a person 4000 years ago who chose a material that was easy to carve and did not split when heated, who used the mould as it became stained by the heat of molten metal being poured into it and who finally threw it away in fury as it broke when the final axe was removed. This story can continue into the present with the discovery of the mould by a farmer while ploughing a field and the ways in which it is used in the museum.

Such a dialogue between a person and an object can be supported and developed by someone who can suggest additional questions and add extra information about an object's context. A good example of this can be seen in the investigation of a Victorian iron and its stand. As well as considering the technology of its manufacture, its social role can also be investigated. Would it have been used by a man or a woman? What does owning an iron say about someone's social status? Does using an iron have the same implications? The ways in which such an apparently mundane object can carry such a range of symbolic meanings is underlined by some particular details of the iron stand that is used in workshops in Marischal Museum. The elaborate, and archetypally Victorian, decoration includes the representation of a bird, a bell, leaves and a ring. To someone familiar with the Glasgow City arms, but to few Aberdonians, this is readily understood and the place where the image of a fish has broken off is easily identified. The presence in an Aberdeen museum of an iron made of cast iron in Glasgow is also a powerful indicator of the effects of the Industrial Revolution.

Conclusions

The aim of the object-handling workshop is to inspire and enlighten children's approaches to an important strand of primary evidence. As excerpts from interviews with children who had taken part in workshops reveals, the opportunity to touch objects and to talk about them lay at the heart of their experiences and enjoyment.

"You really got to try the things out for yourself, to see if they worked for you. Much more helpful than reading it in a book. In a book you can't try to start a fire - with this you can get some sparks. And you can't lift up a lantern if it's on TV and see how light it is."

"If you go in museums, you hardly ever get to touch the stuff and it's boring. But if you get to touch the stuff it's exciting. It helps you to learn more because you're interested. If somebody's talking to you and you're just looking at something you can hardly pay attention. Well, I don't! But if you get to touch it, and they're saying stuff, you follow on and learn."

Contributors

Dr Colleen Batey is Curator of Archaeology at Glasgow Museums. She has excavated widely in northern Scotland and published extensively on Viking and Late Norse Scotland.

Adrian Cox is Post-Excavation Manager and Artefacts Researcher at the Scottish Urban Archaeological Trust. He is a graduate of Leicester University and worked in the English Midlands and Northumberland before joining the Trust in 1988. An experienced excavator, illustrator and finds researcher, Adrian has a long-standing interest in educational and outreach work within archaeology, and has designed educational activities and exhibition material.

Elizabeth Curtis is a primary school teacher and archaeologist. She loves writing, and has recently finished work on a book about the prehistory and early history of Scotland for children. Along with her husband she runs Marischal Museum Young Archaeologists.

Neil Curtis is Assistant Curator of Marischal Museum, University of Aberdeen. With a background in Archaeology, Museum Studies and Education, he is particularly concerned with children's learning with archaeological objects.

Peter Dreghorn MA is a Primary School Development Officer for South Lanarkshire Council. He became interested in the educational link with archaeology as a Biggar Museum Trustee and amateur archaeologist. As well as Glenochar, he has developed further packs for the Kilmartin Valley in Argyll, the Leadhills Railway, The Tarbrax Shale Bing, Kirk o Shotts Church and even the Wishaw House Pet Cemetery.

Marion Fry is a freelance education consultant. Before working as Historic Scotland's Education Officer, Marion taught History, French and Learning Support in Fife. From 1986-1990, she was responsible for creating and developing the Fife History Project, a series of local history folders which are now in every school in Fife.

Barbara Hamilton has worked as the Principal Officer of Education at Perth Museum and Art Gallery since 1990. Her background is in archaeology of the Eastern Mediterranean, educational outreach and theatre in archaeology. Her main pastime involves writing poetry and children's stories, some of which have been published.

Rosemary Hannay graduated from the University of Glasgow in 1976 with an MA in English and Scottish Literature. In 1982 she gained the Manchester University Museums and Galleries Diploma. She then started work in the Scottish Borders at Eyemouth Museum, later working at Kelso Museum and Tweeddale Museum in Peebles. In 1987 she was awarded the Museums Diploma. She is currently Principal Assistant Curator with the Scottish Borders Council Museum Service

Colin McAndrew, Development Fellow with the Scottish Consultative Council on the Curriculum, was Headteacher of Plockton Primary School for many years. He joined SCCC in 1990 and has since worked with the Primary Education Development Project, the Environment and School Initiatives project, and is programme co-ordinator for the Consortium of Institutions for Development and Research in Education in Europe (CIDREE). In 1994 he edited the SCCC Environmental Studies 5-14 Staff Development Support pack.

Alan Paterson's career began in 1974 with a brief spell as a teacher of Business Studies, followed by 11 years working in Aberdeen primary schools. As a primary teacher he developed an interest in Environmental Education and has pursued this further in his current post as Development Officer at Aberdeen Urban Studies Centre, developing his knowledge of environmental matters and developing skills in using the local environment for learning.

Judith Stones is Keeper of Archaeology, Aberdeen City Council, with responsibility for archaeology of all periods within the local authority area, and for the City's archaeological collections. She has excavated many sites, largely of medieval date, mainly in Aberdeen but also in Israel. In the very distant past she trained and worked as a secondary school teacher.

Val Turner has worked as the Shetland Archaeologist for nearly 10 years. She is employed by Shetland Amenity Trust and is responsible for curating all Shetland's monuments! Val is also involved in putting research programmes together and is currently involved in a major excavation and survey programme in the south mainland of Shetland centred on a broch site, Old Scatness. Val is committed to involving the public of all ages in archaeology at various levels, and is always anxious to exchange ideas with like-minded teachers and archaeologists.

Damion Willcock is the Education Officer at Kilmartin House. He has previously worked as a molecular biologist in Edinburgh and as a countryside ranger in East Lothian. He became involved in environmental education through the Young Ornithologists Club and now leads the Great Auks - a joint YOC/YAC club in Mid Argyll.

At home in the past with Tweeddale Museum

HISTORY & ARCHAEOLOGY

SCOTLAND IN DARK AGE BRITAIN
Barbara Crawford (ed.)
1 898218 61 7 172pp pb

SCOTTISH BURGH SURVEYS

Historic Musselburgh
1 898218 44 7 c108pp

Historic Dunblane
1 898218 43 9 c96pp

Historic Aberdeen
1 898218 39 0 c192pp

Historic Coupar Angus
1 898218 48 X

Historic Stornoway
1 898218 49 8

Historic Dalkeith
1 898218 50 1

Historic Melrose
1 898218 51 X

Historic Nairn
1 898218 52 8

Historic Kirkcaldy
1 898218 38 2 96pp

Historic Stanraer
1 898218 41 2 96pp

Historic Cumnock
1 898218 40 4 72pp

Historic Hamilton
1 898218 42 0 96pp

Selected Titles from
SCOTTISH CHILDREN'S PRESS

DISCOVER SCOTLAND'S HISTORY
A D Cameron
1 898218 76 5 256pp pb

SCOTLAND IN ROMAN TIMES
Antony Kamm
1 899827 14 5 64pp pb

WALLACE, BRUCE, AND THE WAR OF INDEPENDENCE
Antony Kamm
Illustrated by Jennifer Campbell
1 899827 15 3 64pp pb